CARING

for those in CRISIS

CARING
for those in CRISIS

Facing Ethical Dilemmas with
Patients and Families

Kenneth P. Mottram

Brazos Press
Grand Rapids, Michigan

© 2007 by Kenneth P. Mottram

Published by Brazos Press
a division of Baker Publishing Group
P.O. Box 6287, Grand Rapids, MI 49516-6287
www.brazospress.com

Printed in the United States of America

Library of Congress Cataloging-in-Publication Data
Mottram, Kenneth P., 1953—
    Caring for those in crisis : facing ethical dilemmas with patients and families / Kenneth P. Mottram.
      p.   cm.
    Includes bibliographical references.
    ISBN 10: 1-58743-191-2 (pbk.)
    ISBN 978-158743-191-3 (pbk.)
    1. Pastoral medicine. 2. Sick—Pastoral counseling of. 3. Patients—Pastoral counseling of. 4. Church work with the sick. 5. Church work with families. 6. Medicine—Religious aspects—Christianity. 7. Medical ethics. I. Title.
BV4335.M68 2007
259′4—dc22
                                    2006024090

Contents

Acknowledgments

A project of this nature cannot be completed without the help and support of a wide variety of persons. I want to express my thanks to the many physicians, staff, and hospital administrators I have had the privilege to learn from and serve with in the care of patients and families. They are representative of the wider family of dedicated and compassionate health-care providers found across this country and around the world.

Throughout my years of training I was privileged to be associated with a variety of educators who were very helpful in furthering my understanding of bioethics and medical ethics. Mel Friedman, M.D., proctored my first doctoral seminar on medical ethics. Ann Cook, Ph.D., and Helena Hoas, Ph.D., from the National Rural Bioethics Project of the University of Montana, Missoula, gave their personal time in helping me understand ethical dilemmas and caregiver concerns. At Canadian Southern Baptist Seminary, Jimmy Cobb, Ph.D., became a friend and valued support as he critiqued my writing and offered new areas of possible research. Dr. Ronald Hornecker at Golden Gate Baptist Theological Seminary gave me the courage to reach higher in my academic pursuit. The inspiration, encouragement, and prayers of Eugene H. Peterson will remain as a personal and professional joy and honored privilege.

There have been many pastors and chaplain colleagues over the years who have provided support and mentoring relationships that are so important to the living of a life that endures crisis and the sometimes catastrophic events that mark our human pilgrimage. I remember especially Rev. Dallas French, Rev. Thomas Hastings, Rev. Herb Luebeck, Rev. Robert Starburg, and Rev. Milton Gire.

Finally, I want to thank my family and children for their encouragement and love. Russ, Rob, and Krista, you are the reason I write. Susan, you are the joy of my life.

This book is dedicated to mentor and friend Rev. Paul J. Taylor, who, with his wife Marilyn, taught me the compassion of a chaplain and who died leaving a legacy of grateful patients and families.

All names and events used in this book have been altered but are based on personal experience.

> "This above all: to thine own self be true, and it must follow
> as the night the day, thou canst not then
> be false to any man."
>
> Shakespeare, *Hamlet*

Foreword

"Medical ethics" strikes most of us as remotely academic—something that professors lecture on while their students take notes and prepare to write papers or sit for exams. Nothing could be farther from the truth. Medical ethics is a shorthand phrase for dealing with the emotional complexities and the baffling decisions so many of us will have to make in the uncongenial, impersonal setting of a room in a hospital. Unprepared and distraught we are faced with a physician whom we have never seen who is an expert, or so we think, in matters of life and death. The expert presents us, the amateurs, with a decision. At best we are confused, at worst distraught.

Crisis. The decisive moment when things either get better or worse. Sometimes we get a say in the decision that may or may not effect the "better or worse." Crisis plunges us into life and death matters; there is nothing abstract or theoretical about a crisis decision, and there is no "right" decision that we can look up in a textbook.

Crisis is an interruption of the ordinary. We have no way of anticipating it: car accidents, encounters with a grizzly, attempted suicides, terrorist attacks. We get the news while washing the dishes, mowing the lawn, vacationing in Bermuda, sitting in a classroom, writing a letter, fixing a faucet. We get no warning, either emotional or mental. What do we do? We are clueless, prayerless.

Kenneth Mottram spends his days (and sometimes nights!) working with men and women caught in the crisis of making life and death decisions for their spouses and children, parents, and friends who are in crisis. His primary field of work is the hospital emergency room. But while crisis, by definition, cannot be prepared for—it is unanticipated and the details are unique—there are some preparations that can be made. He helps us make them.

He does it by taking us with him into the crisis experiences that he faces in his work, telling us the stories so we can experience beforehand for ourselves in imagination and prayer the world of crisis. He gives us an orientation in the intricate emotions and multi-layered family dynamics that are almost always involved in a medical crisis. But more significantly, he provides an orientation in the Christian and biblical world that provides the larger reality in which we live and die. With his careful and detailed guidance in the ways that Christians pray and listen, care for and love one another, he expands the walls of the hospital room or physician's consulting room into an immense world of God's truth, the community of faith that has generations of experience in wise living and wise dying. If he doesn't give us answers on what is right and wrong in particular circumstances, he greatly enlarges the scope of our understanding beyond the crisis as it is defined by medical options. He gathers us into the community of men and women who are prepared to live with life and death decisions in terms of repentance and forgiveness and hope as Jesus lived (and lives) them among us.

This is not a special interest book—all of us are liable to have to deal unexpectedly with the issues presented so humanly and accessibly here. Pastors and their families, doctors and nurses, and almost everyone else I can think of, will find help and wisdom here.

But there is also an element of urgency that reverberates through the pages of this book. We live in a time when health care is increasingly depersonalized. It is more often than not reduced to the secular and political considerations that dominate the field. Dr. Mottram expands the imagination of people of faith and prepares us to deal with the crisis, when and if it comes, in ways that give dignity to our values and the considerations of life and death under the aspect of eternity.

Eugene H. Peterson

1

Meeting an Ethical Dilemma

I saw Jack for the first time in the Emergency Room, when he was there to minister to a family in distress. He was a big man wearing a red-checked flannel shirt. He had kind eyes and looked worried. He introduced himself, told me he was representing a church, and related that he had received a frantic phone call from a family from his congregation just a few minutes earlier. The family had been notified that an elderly woman had been hit by a truck while crossing the street. They were upset and heading for the hospital. They wanted Jack to join them. I was a staff chaplain at the medical center and was paged to the ER to respond to a trauma being brought in by our air ambulance. I met Jack as he stepped through the door. In the ER the flight crew had just arrived with a frail eighty-five-year-old lady. They quickly transferred her to the trauma room and were rapt in the process of initial diagnostic testing and life-sustaining interventions. The crew had intubated her in the field by putting a breathing tube into her lungs and "bagging" her until a ventilator could be connected at the hospital. Now she was receiving IV fluid and blood pressure support. Tests revealed she had multiple fractures of her legs and hip. Persons on the scene related that she had been thrown several feet upon impact. In the midst of the chaos, and with Jack and I both wondering how this accident could have happened, five other members of the family arrived. They recognized Jack and went right up to him. He embraced them and held several of them together in a group with arms clasped. I could tell they knew him as a friend and as a supportive individual. Jack was a teaching elder of their church. The senior pastor was out of town. This family crisis, in this hospital, on this day was going to be handled by him. They needed spiritual and faith support, and he was the only leader of their church in town.

I showed them to our family support room and reported that the ER physician would want to speak with them as soon as the patient was stable. Jack immediately called the family to prayer, and everyone cried openly as they interceded on Mildred's behalf. I prayed with them as we called upon God to keep Mildred safe and to give the ER staff wisdom and guidance. Mildred's survival was uncertain. As the family introduced themselves to me Mildred's daughter Bonnie was particularly emotional. She was perhaps in her mid-fifties, pleasant-looking and friendly, but with eye-lines that made me realize that she had lived some difficult years. Jack took me aside later to let me know that Bonnie was single, lived with her mother, and was financially dependent upon her. He knew that if Mildred died Bonnie would have to leave her home (since she would not be able to make the payments) *as well as* grieve the loss of her most significant relationship. Jack also said that Bonnie had lost three other family members by death in the last year. The cumulative effect of all the deaths had taken a toll on her. Jack knew that she was barely holding her life together.

It is my practice as a hospital spiritual caregiver to keep the family abreast of the events occurring in the trauma room. One of the worst things about being in one of these situations is the unknown. We're fearful of what may be happening, and we can't be by the side of the one we love. I made many trips to the trauma room and then back to the family to describe the variety of interventions being done for Mildred. Four physicians were consulting on the patient, including an ER doctor, a thoracic surgeon, an orthopedic surgeon, and a brain surgeon. Her room was continually crowded with ten or more ER staff. Three RNs attended her, and the respiratory therapist was monitoring her oxygen levels and the ventilator. Various X-ray and phlebotomist "techs" rotated in and out of the trauma room as they took pictures and gathered blood samples. The hospital supervisor (the RN administrator) was taking notes and charting all the activities being yelled at him from around Mildred's bedside. As I listened to the physicians and RNs crowded around this little lady, it became clear that they didn't expect her to live. On top of the multiple pelvic and leg fractures, Mildred had experienced a head injury, with slow bleeding into her cranial cavities. Her old chart, on file with our medical records department, added preexisting conditions of diabetes and a slow-moving lung cancer to the list of risk factors. Her system was already taxed *before* this accident.

When the ER physician explained all this to the family and suggested that Mildred might not survive her injuries, Bonnie became hysterical. Everything had happened too quickly. It was too sudden. There were no chances to say good-bye. Surely the physicians had missed something! Jack tried to calm her, and with a very mature, godly attitude, gathered the family for prayer again. It brought tears to my eyes to see a family faced with a life-changing tragedy bow before God in humble dependence. Jack prayed, "O Father, we don't understand this terrible event. We ask for your intervention to save Mildred's life. Give us a miracle, Father God. Help the doctors and nurses to be guided by your Spirit. We're thankful that Mildred is one of your children and has a place in your kingdom. And we trust you, Lord, as our strength and refuge. But we ask that you spare her life at this time. In the name of Jesus our Lord, Amen."

On his second visit with the family, the ER physician came into the room looking subdued and worried in a professional sort of way. When he spoke, his voice was filled with concern. He spoke softly as he asked the family to make a decision regarding aggressive care for Mildred. He explained again that Mildred would probably not survive her injuries, but that she might live for a few days or weeks. Options for her care included: (1) withdraw support and allow Mildred to die within a few hours; (2) continue with life support and transfer Mildred to a larger medical center several hundred miles away; or (3) continue life support and keep Mildred at our hospital and close to local family, where she would have family visitors but with perhaps fewer specialists to manage her difficult pulmonary, brain, and orthopedic injuries, along with her cancer and diabetes. I spoke openly with Jack about my concerns regarding the financial burdens any further treatment would place upon the family and Bonnie. Multiple days in an intensive care unit (ICU), with multiple physicians consulting, would bankrupt Bonnie, and with the outcome still being Mildred's death. As a chaplain I'm not usually so open with family about financial costs, because it always comes across as "insensitive" or is perceived as not respecting the value of human life. But with Jack able to support the family and to be a more consoling and familiar voice of reason, I felt justified to raise the "money issue." Often I have seen families devastated by astronomical medical bills after just trying to save the life of someone they love and can't bear to be without.

But Bonnie could think only about losing her mother. Even given the knowledge that her mother would not survive more than a few weeks, she told the ER physician to continue full aggressive support and what are sometimes termed "heroic measures." Though other members of the family were uncertain Bonnie was making the right choice, they didn't want to offend her. I related to Jack that Mildred's Christian commitments should make the decision-making process easier and should give us confidence in allowing her to "go and be with her Lord." After all, she had probably thought about meeting Jesus many times in her life. It is surely our hope as Christian people. But Bonnie wanted to hang on. Mildred died after sixteen days in the ICU. She never regained consciousness. The family never mentioned to me the impact of the resulting medical bills, but there is no doubt they were substantial and crippling in outcome for this middle-income family.

Life-and-death decisions like this one are faced by families daily in our hospitals and medical centers. Over the last eight years it has been my ministry to be a hospital spiritual caregiver or chaplain. In the first hours when life hangs in the balance, it has been my role to provide crisis support for fearful families and loved ones. Often I am with families as critical care physicians explain the risks the patient faces and the choices family members have regarding quality-of-life issues and whether to use heroic measures of life support. The role of a chaplain is difficult in these situations. You can't make the decisions for people. You have to keep all the options open for the family and help them through the maze of choices, all of which may seem too hard to face. A spiritual caregiver has to be honest in the midst of it all. What is happening to the patient and family is real. It is hard stuff. The tendency we have as Christian people of faith is to say, "It is going to be OK." But it may not be. Lives may be affected in ways that will forever change living patterns or family relationships. Or someone might die. It is always hard to think or speak the "death" word. We have a hard time thinking that we will lose someone we love. But life is real, and death is a part of life. And so a spiritual caregiver walks this ground that is authentic, honest, real, and sometimes devastating. Tears are often inevitable.

It has also been my role to help families with the ethical issues involved in making decisions that affect whether a person will live or die. Such questions as "Does my father have a say in how he wants to end his life?" and "If my religion prohibits that treatment, can I decline it?" and "If the physician recommends a procedure, do I have to follow her advice?" all hinge on patient and family rights and are the new questions of controversy in the contemporary medical center. In my contacts with the many families who have faced these issues, they invariably count the experience as one of the worst they have ever had to confront. Sometimes they are at odds with the physicians they have always trusted in the past. At times like these the loving support and objective counsel of a Christian leader is great comfort and a welcomed strength.

Jack was not ordained professional clergy, and yet he found himself—because of his commitment to the church and his church family—in the position of "pastoral adviser," Christian advocate, and spiritual caregiver for Mildred's family. He was a blessing and a support for this family in the midst of one of the most frightening experiences of their lives. He brought the faith of the family to the forefront and modeled human dependence upon God in uncertain circumstances as he united the family in prayer for Mildred's life. Church pastors and clergy have often found themselves supporting the members of their congregation in times of crisis, whether at the hospital bedside, or when death occurs, or at times when difficult decision making is required. But in our contemporary life situation, neighbors, good friends and family, and other Christian mentors also may be thrust into that role. It is an unfamiliar place for most of us, and that is why this book is important. It is critical that pastors, Christian counselors, seminarians, and other church leaders educate themselves in medical ethics and hospital spiritual support, and that is what I attempt to do in the following pages. The hospital setting is intimidating, and physicians come to a crisis with great expertise, unfamiliar terminology, and a variety of personal preferences and concerns that can overwhelm those just seeking to cope with and understand a sudden accident. To have a spiritual support person nearby as an advocate is a gift from God in these circumstances.

Inevitably in such emotion-laden situations a variety of moral or ethical concerns arise having to do with the family and the patient. After all, everyone is dealing with the potential death of someone they love. And that person in jeopardy has a unique way of looking at life and personal wishes about his or her life. Most of us in our media-oriented society have been exposed to television dramas like *ER* or the various *CSI* shows with their graphic portrayals of death and medical procedures. We have been exposed as a culture to the varieties of issues and decisions that confront doctors and nurses in their practices. We have read news articles on government intervention in "pulling the plug" on someone at death's door, and squabbles where family members disagree about a medical condition or outcome. Certainly the terrible tragedy in Florida in which a family's disagreements about Terri Schiavo's care went to the courts—and even to the U.S. Congress—have touched a nerve in us. As a result we have strong feelings regarding our own care, and many of us have determined ahead of time how we want things to go if we find ourselves in that position—that is, if we have our choice. As never before in our country people want to enter the scene and make their viewpoints known. In today's hospitals, similar decisions are made by physicians and families daily, and ethical issues abound.

When Jack responded to Mildred's accident he was suddenly thrown into the midst of a host of choices to be made. Because the choices all have unknown positive or negative ramifications they are sometimes called *dilemmas*. A dilemma is a situation in which a difficult choice has to be made between two alternatives, especially when a decision either way will bring undesirable consequences. Those making the decision are uncertain in balancing one decision—with its consequences—against another. In Jack's case he was confronted with Bonnie's grief issues and the potential of another devastating loss versus Mildred's approaching death and the potential undue suffering that she might endure. Many persons express concern about allowing a loved one to suffer. Should Jack support the doctor and his prognosis that Mildred would not survive, or should he support Bonnie and attempt to *ready* her for a death perhaps weeks away? Should Bonnie's issues take precedent since she will have the longer life? And what about withdrawing aggressive support and just letting Mildred die within a few hours? Is this what Christians do? Is this what Jesus would do? In Mildred's situation there is the concern about *rightness* and *wrongness* of an action.

Then there's the matter of the financial aspect of care. Is it ethical to talk money when someone's life is on the line? I didn't know what the family would think about my raising this issue. But Jack knew the family well. If Mildred or they had ever expressed strong feelings regarding futile life support or draining of family savings, a personal pastor might know them. And then, finally, the issue of transferring Mildred to another specialist hospital for better care is another important consideration. If Mildred is to die as expected, would she want to die away from the majority of her family and friends, or with them by her side as much as possible? When death approaches, suddenly specialized medical treatment might not be the highest priority. Unfortunately, this *human* aspect of final decision making is sometimes forgotten; weeks later the realization might come to the family that Mildred died alone. Regrets may follow.

Bonnie and her family were faced with all of these issues as the decisions about Mildred's care were made. They were blessed to have Jack as their spiritual support and Christian advocate through the process. We can know that not all situations have outcomes that are tidy, clean, or without difficulties. Unfortunately, medical science is also an art, and there are always uncertainties.

Two Choices, Two Families

A twenty-eight-year-old mother with a husband and three young children was brought to our hospital one day after overdosing on Tylenol. She had not been found for twenty-four hours. Her husband and kids had left for work and school the morning before and didn't think anything about the fact that she slept through the entire evening. But the next morning she still did not awaken. At that point they knew something was amiss. When the ambulance arrived, her respiration was faint and her pupils were fixed and dilated—often a symptom of brain damage. She was intubated and placed on a ventilator in the intensive care unit. It was a desperate situation the next two days as the ICU staff and other caregivers watched her two girls and her boy, all in elementary school, stand at the bedside of their mom, asking whether she would be well someday. Many of the nurses were in tears. After three days of no improvement, a neurological examination showed that significant brain damage had occurred. The husband, the neurologist, and I gathered for a family conference to decide how to proceed. The doctor informed the husband that the patient *might* survive if the present course were continued, but that she would not be the same person. She would probably need institutionalization. On the other hand, there was no way to predict just how high (or low) a level of functioning she would achieve over time. Given this dire news, the husband—who had few resources and was facing an uncertain economic future—decided that his wife would not have wanted to be handicapped or to live in a vegetative state, so he chose to withdraw support. The breathing machine was disconnected and other blood pressure meds curtailed so that the patient was without heroic medical support. Comfort measures were instituted to keep the young mother as pain-free as possible. She lived for two days and then died. A surviving husband and three children were devastated at the sudden change in their lives. It never became clear whether the mother had purposely tried to end her life, or if the overdose was accidental.

Only ten or twelve weeks later a similar case came to our hospital. A female in her late forties attempted suicide by ingesting some Tylenol. The drug had been in her system for more than twenty-four hours. Her husband called 911, and our helicopter went to pick her up at a rural location. She was foaming at the mouth and had a bluish tone to her skin, according to the husband. She was settled into our ICU when four or five other family arrived, including her mother and father, who were strong Christian people. They were happy to have me there to pray with them and offer spiritual support. Several pastor friends lived near their home, but all were a hundred miles away from the hospital. When this family sat down with the same neurologist and heard the same news, they were struck by the fact that a decision had to be made in such a short time. They left the room and went outside the hospital to talk about it with one another and to pray. After nearly an hour, they came back with the decision to continue life support, regardless of the potential for permanent impairment and the possibility of institution-alization. I remember that many of the ICU staff felt that this was the wrong choice and that the family didn't understand the ramifications of their decision. But much to the surprise of everyone, the patient later recovered enough to live independently again! She was not the same as before the surgery but was able to live an acceptable quality of life that was a joy for her family and meaningful in its own right.

I had a wise clinical supervisor during my chaplain training who said, "In the hospital some people will die that you never expect to die, and some will live that you never expect to live." Many times decisions are not easily discernible. Why is it that one family holds on and "feels in their bones" that a young woman will live? And why must another young mother depart the children who need her and have relied upon her? Sometimes the best medical advice can turn out to be a nightmare, and at other times decisions made that confound the medical world turn out to be a triumph of faith and a sign of God's presence in our lives.

Both of these families were faced with several decisions. Although the patients' overdoses were life-threatening upon admission, the physi-cians were able to stabilize both cases, *but* with concerns about qual-ity of life. The families needed to make a decision about the patients' wishes for quality of life and to struggle with the idea that the decision they made might bring long-term suffering for the patients as well as for themselves. The decision to sustain life might have been perceived as "doing harm" in the long run. Once again the financial aspects of initial treatment and long-term care might have had an impact on the decisions made in these two cases. I think the husband of the first patient was overwhelmed by the possibility of long-term complications and bearing financial responsibility. Finally, deeply embedded within the decision-making process is the heart-wrenching realization for these families that life is precious and that *their* decision will have an effect on whether that life continues or physically ends. It's a frightening place to have to be.

Fast Decisions, Uncertain Results

A particularly difficult situation often occurs in the ER when snap decisions must be made, with families already upset and distressed. Such was the case one morning when an elderly lady named Lula was found by her caregiver collapsed on the floor of her home. Susan, a home health aide employed to watch over Lula, saw that her eyes were open but that she was unable to respond and was having trouble breathing. Her breaths came in gasps, and her color was changing. Susan called 911. The ambulance crew responded quickly, put an oxygen mask on her, and rushed her to the hospital.

Upon arrival the ER physician set up EKG and O_2 monitors, started an IV, and checked her blood pressure. Almost immediately Lula's condition declined, and she started to go into respiratory arrest. In a couple of minutes her daughter Joyce and Joyce's husband Tom arrived. I met them, told them Lula was being attended to, and took them to the Family Room, where they could have some privacy while waiting to hear from the doctor. They were both very emotional, concerned with what could be happening with their mother so suddenly. When I went back to the trauma room to tell the ER doc that the family had arrived, there were eight staff in the room and a lot of hurried movement. They were getting ready to intubate Lula. To let Joyce and Tom know the extent of what was now happening and to ready them for possibly worse news, I went back and reported the possibility of a ventilator intervention. Joyce immediately said, "No! She wouldn't want that. She doesn't want to be a vegetable." Seeing the adamant nature of Joyce's response made me wonder if Lula had thought about this happening to her, that she might have spoken to her family about this eventuality, and that she could have some written living will or advance directive on file. If that is the case, the ER doctor should know.

I reported Joyce's words to Dr. John, and a quick conference was held. Dr. John was clear with the family about his speaking to the patient. He related that he spoke to Lula loudly and seriously, his face inches from hers: "We need to put you on a breathing machine. If you don't have it, you will die. What do you want me to do?" Lula, with eyes half shut and half open, barely able to breathe, her body heaving, mouthed a weak "yes" and nodded her head in the affirmative. Dr. John quickly explained this to Joyce and Tom and said that he needed to get back to Lula as soon as possible. There was no time to search for a living will. He left.

I stayed with Joyce and Tom and attempted to explain "informed consent" to them. I told them it was good that Lula was able to respond to Dr. John at all, and that the breathing machine is often used to just "take the pressure off the body's resources" and allow a patient time to "get over the hump" of a physical stress. If a patient is of sound mind and able to make their own decisions—just as Lula did—then the family should feel comfortable with the decision. But Joyce and Tom were not comfortable. They were still upset and wanting to honor the wishes of their mother. Joyce kept saying, "She does not want to be on a ventilator. She has said it many times. I don't want her to be angry with me." Lula was intubated in the ER and taken to the ICU. At this time there was no guarantee that she would survive.

Sadly, Lula did not survive. She spent a week in the ICU, was able to get off the ventilator, and was moved to a floor room, but she was so medicated and weak that she could not go home. She wasted away in our skilled-care nursing home for two more weeks before finally dying. When I spoke to Joyce over the phone several days after Lula's death, she just said, "I feel like I put Mom through a month of suffering that she shouldn't have had to endure." Lula had indeed been on a ventilator several other times in her later years and, with her progressive lung disease, had spoken to her family often about not wanting to be on a ventilator again. Joyce wondered about Lula's response to the ER doctor on that fateful morning. His question to her was, "We need to put you on a breathing machine. If you don't have it, you will die. What do you want me to do?" When she whispered "yes" and nodded her head, could she have been saying "I know, and I am ready to die"? Joyce said that her mother was a strong Christian believer, a woman of courage who was unafraid of death and looking forward to heaven.

Joyce said that she continues to believe that the doctor made the wrong decision. On the phone that day she expressed a lot of anger about how things had been handled. Decisions had to be made and made quickly.

To be fair to Dr. John we must remember that ER physicians are in the business of saving lives, and they save many of them. Their world is marked by crisis and extreme intervention. And most often families and patients are grateful. But occasionally an unusual situation like Lula's arises. The choice in the height of the crisis seemed obvious to Dr. John, that is, to err on the side of saving a life. Legally, that is the high-percentage choice. But the good and right and honoring choice was not the choice made that day. Lula's choice was, in effect, disregarded, and the family left angry. Would it have been different if an advocate for Lula had been there? If there had been someone less emotionally involved than Joyce or Tom, but supporting what was known of Lula's wishes, perhaps she could have passed away with greater dignity.

A Need for Advocacy

Through my involvements in these family traumas I have experienced the dissonance of the hospital. I have seen the impersonal nature of the institutional setting. I have seen families struggle with questions that seem to have no clear answer. I have ministered to families in a variety of crises. In it all I have developed a passion to bring Christian leaders to a better understanding of the life of the contemporary medical center. This book will help pastors, Christian counselors, and other church leaders who will find themselves ministering in hospitals and at sickbeds. Ethical dilemmas occur daily in our medical centers, and the new discipline of medical ethics is quickly becoming the way of talking about the decision-making process. Yet many Christian leaders have not been exposed to medical ethics and its terminology. Ethics as a course of study sounds complicated and intellectually elitist to the average Christian. But nothing could be further from the truth. I am convinced that Christian leaders and others training for ministry need to be informed about the types of ethical issues commonly faced by patients and their families, and to educate themselves in the terminology of medical ethics. For many of us, these are uncharted waters, and feelings of inadequacy run deep.

I am also convinced that health-care workers need the voice of spiritual leaders as a guide in difficult situations and to serve as a reminder of ultimate values. It is my experience that many physicians welcome the counsel of reflective spiritual leaders. Some physicians have told me that their job is easier if someone is available to the family to help in the education process and to interpret hard-to-grasp therapies. And if a family can be supported spiritually, they respond to medical caregivers with more openness and less suspicion.

Finally, those forced to face ethical dilemmas requiring decision making often ask for help and counsel. They are like "sheep without a shepherd" (Mark 6:34). It is my conviction that health-care chaplains fill an important role in supporting families in crisis but are insufficient for the task of patient advocacy and family support. Many times I relied upon pastors or elders to communicate what needed to be said to upset families. As spiritual leaders, each one of us has a duty to teach and pastor *our* flocks, those *we* know and who know *us,* and to advocate for them with the fullest counsel of God available to us.

To this end you will find in the following chapters a practical orientation to the contemporary hospital ministry situation. You will be introduced to the development of medical ethics as a discipline and to several important ethics principles that guide decision making in the hospital setting when ethical dilemmas occur. Your personal awareness will be challenged as you discover your own operational value system and realize that past personal experiences influence your approach to medical decisions and how you counsel others. Through the eyes of an experienced hospital spiritual caregiver you will be exposed to a variety of very common ethical dilemmas and will be given a process to help in communicating with all stakeholders in reaching a resolution. The medical understanding of spirituality is covered so that readers will have an idea of how physicians and medical caregivers approach spirituality and human wellness. Finally, some specifically Christian distinctives of decision making will be proposed, and Christian interventions discussed. It is my hope and passion that readers will become equipped in this new ministry of ethics advocacy and that the kingdom of God will benefit from the result.

In the modern medical center, life is daily held in the balance. Real people are being asked to make decisions that affect them and their loved ones at the deepest level. Real love for persons who might suddenly be taken from them by trauma or terminal illness sometimes clouds decision-making processes of family members forced into awful choices by the uncertainties of life. In this chaos of real life, an available and willing Christian with a godly calling can bring informed counsel and true support. It is a needed ministry in our changing world.

2

Orientation to Medical Ethics

To begin the journey of equipping ourselves for hospital ministry and patient advocacy, first we need to look at the history of medical ethics and get some basic terminology into our vocabulary. The ways physicians and medical professionals look at morality and how they speak about it are probably unfamiliar to many of us involved in Christian leadership. If you are like me, you were exposed to some sort of ethics class in college, seminary, or other schooling. Usually such classes focus on classical ethics or philosophical ethics but don't touch the sort of ethics application that you will find in dealing with ethical dilemmas in a medical or health-care context. I was surprised to discover that even many medical schools just started including an ethics class for physicians in the past few years. Until that time many physicians came out of medical school unprepared to deal with the types of patient and family value conflicts they would encounter in their practices. So as Christian leaders we are not alone in this new field of education. But we need to learn and to have a basic idea of what has brought ethics into the forefront of medical discussions. So we begin.

The first thing to know about medical ethics is that *anyone* can understand ethics and *everyone* faces it. Our lives are woven around it. It is nothing that must be left to the classroom, medical doctors, or the scholarly elite. All of us have at some time in our lives read something

or seen something that exposed us to the idea of ethics. Sometimes
we meet the subject in the workplace or sometimes in a community
volunteer organization. A list of "principles of action" or an organizational code of ethics surfaces to guide the board members or workplace
employees in their interactions, relationships, or performance. We get
the feeling that ethics has to do with *character* or *upstanding conduct*.
And, in fact, this is indeed what ethics is about.

Ethics is a word that fundamentally speaks to morality. In fact the
English word often used in tandem with medical ethics, *bioethics*, is
a combined form of the Greek words *bios*, meaning "life," and *ethica*,
which comes from the noun *etheos*, meaning "what relates to character."[1] And so bioethics (or medical ethics) is the study of "life character" by definition. It is no surprise, then, that we often see ethics as
a discipline referred to as "moral philosophy." Christian people have
always been interested in moral issues related to lifestyle and personal
choices. As we read scripture we seek to discover what actions are
right for our lives and what actions are wrong. We want to know how
to live our lives in harmony with God's will, creation, and people. We
are concerned about righteousness and justice and God's moral law. In
effect, we are concerned about *ethics* and the living of a successful life
of moral character in God's world and among God's people. So ethics
is bound up in our lives and is a part of our personal philosophy as
Christian people.

Some schools of ethical thought prefer to draw a distinction between
ethics and morality/morals. From their perspective, ethics is to be
viewed as more theoretical, that is, the *study* of the right and the good,
whereas morality is to be viewed as personally specific and practical,
that is, the *living out* of what one considers to be right and good.[2]
Although such distinctions may provide some helpfulness in various
contexts, to draw a clean line between ethics and morality is clearly
impossible. Ethics concerns choices for living life, and therein finds
expression as both noun and verb. Every choice is a moral choice.

The Historical Roots of Medical Ethics

The earliest human writings contained elements of discerning right
from wrong. Certainly the earliest Judeo-Christian writings contained
much having to do with law and moral living, the Ten Commandments
being foremost in importance. One would think that the Hebrew scriptures would provide the seeds for the development of our contem-

porary views of medical ethics. Today biblical ethics is a continually growing body of study. However, in the modern study of medical ethics a gulf developed, separating authoritative Christian writings from the literature of medical ethics. What we find is that the development of medical ethics followed a different family tree than that of Christian ethics. The trunk of the medical ethics tree is rooted in Greek philosophical thought.

Although several early Greek philosophers, including Thales of Miletus (640–546 BC), Socrates, and Plato (both fifth century BC), provided important foundational theses for ethical thinking, perhaps the most notable Greek philosopher affecting contemporary medical ethics understanding was Hippocrates of Cos (ca. 460–c. 377 BC). Hippocrates played a fundamental role in shaping the earliest *principles* of ethics of Western medicine, and continues to be part of the discussions and modern debate on medical ethics in our day. The Hippocratic Oath is a brief document that has been used for centuries to inspire physicians to selfless service and high ethical standards. A part of the Hippocratic Oath (see the Appendix for the full text) states, "I will use treatment to help the sick according to my ability and judgment, but never with a view to injury or wrongdoing."[3] This statement has provided the foundation for the ethical principles of *beneficence* (the duty to do good) and *nonmaleficence* (the duty to do no harm). These dual precepts became the marching orders of physicians and health-care practitioners from the time of Hippocrates into the modern era. Physicians were encouraged to exemplify those persons who hold themselves above personal gain or political expediency, and the best of them reflected well the principles that Hippocrates made famous. Physicians were trusted by those who depended on them to have their best welfare at heart and to do the right thing in seeking to promote health and wholeness.

Throughout the centuries there can be no doubt that human nature, being what it is, fell short of this ideal as some physicians did not hold to the Hippocratic Oath and innocent persons were compromised. In recent times the medical indiscretions of physicians in World War II Germany became the first large-scale medical travesty to shock the health-care culture of the twentieth century and raise the red flag of concern for the welfare of innocent people. This was to be the birthplace of our modern interest in medical ethics.

For the first time in modern history medical experiments were conducted with no thought for the protection of the patient, in abhorrent violation of the duty of the physician to "do good." Instead physicians' actions led to the mass destruction of humanity. One historical analyst captures the significance of this event by writing: "The discipline of bioethics is dated by most historians to begin with the events of the 1960s. However, I maintain that it was under the penumbra of events of the 1940s that it emerged, especially the Nuremberg medical trials. . . . The trials provided the wedge which allowed wider negotiations about the medical moral order to occur and were integral conditions for the construction of bioethics."[4]

There was a lot of soul searching being done when the events of World War II came to light. People began to notice and document events that raised questions about the actions of medical professionals. However, though the physicians of World War II provided an initial wake-up call, three other highly publicized—and humanly abusive—research projects added subsequent fuel to the bioethics fire.

The first project came to light in 1963 at the Jewish Chronic Disease Hospital in Brooklyn, New York. There chronically ill elderly patients were purposely injected with live cancer cells as a means to discover whether the cells would multiply. The concern that eventually came to the attention of the public is that no patient or family consent was obtained for these experimental injections. These elderly patients had no idea that they were being injected with live cancer cells and used in an experimental fashion.[5]

The second research project was discovered in 1965 and had to do with a U.S. Public Health Service study of syphilis among poor, uneducated, black men in Tuskegee, Alabama. Penicillin had by then become readily available for treatment of syphilis, but the researchers did not tell the subjects that treatment was available. Once again personal rights were violated and the suffering of patients was allowed for the supposed future benefits of medical research. In 1972 the project was officially declared "ethically unjustified" by a task force from the Department of Health, Education, and Welfare.[6]

A third ill-conceived project involved the Willowbrook State School in New York in 1967. There mentally retarded children were given hepatitis injections in hopes of finding ways to mitigate damage done by the disease. Although families were given information about the study, the consent was determined to have an element of coercion, "as it was difficult to gain placement in the institution and if parents consented to research participation the children were admitted both to the project and to the institution."[7] So parents enrolled their children, assuming their children's health and welfare was going to be a high priority of the school. This was not the case.

These three examples of research projects, all breaching the dignity of the patient, and all coming to public awareness in the 1960s, served to drive an interest in bioethics by medical professionals and, unfortunately, also built upon an already rising public distrust of the medical profession. In larger hospitals ethics committees were formed, and in professional journals more and more writing was surfacing on ethics-related topics.

Another leap toward today's understanding of medical ethics occurred in 1977 with the publication of Tom Beauchamp and James Childress's *Principles of Biomedical Ethics*, which was the first book to lay claim to being a common disciplinary standard in the new field.[8] The impetus for their work came from the medical field itself, as the development of new technology and new life-sustaining procedures raised issues of ethical importance. An example of this new technology was the dialysis machine. Hemodialysis was able to keep patients without kidney function alive, but there were initially not enough dialysis machines to go around. Questions arose, such as: "Which patients should be offered the new treatment of the new dialysis machines?" "Which patients will be left without dialysis and die?"

A second development was use of the ventilator in life-support measures. Ventilators came to be more widespread, and suddenly even persons with brain death could be kept alive as life-giving oxygen was pumped into their lungs to sustain bodily organs. But then the questions became "How long should they be kept alive?" and "What criteria should be used to declare death?"

Third, organ donation became a new possibility. If organs can be kept functioning with a ventilator, why can't they be transplanted into another person in a life-saving intervention? And what criteria were to be used to guide the process of candidate selection? Some people would inevitably die, while others would be saved. These issues and others entered the public eye and presented a need to discuss health-care decisions, impending federal legislation, and decision-making authority.

In their book Beauchamp and Childress set forth four operational principles to be used as working tools for "evaluating and adjudicating case-based ethical dilemmas."[9] The four principles they proposed are: beneficence, nonmaleficence (both from the Hippocratic Oath), autonomy, and justice. These four principles are well known to all physicians and have become the unofficial criteria for reflecting upon and resolving medical ethics dilemmas. To begin our journey into the world of medical ethics we need to have a working understanding of some basic terminology. We will begin by defining these four principles and briefly examining their use in ethical decision making.

Four Common Medical Ethics Principles

1. Beneficence: the duty to "do good."

In medical care the basic principle and motivating factor for most physicians is summed up in this word, which emphasizes the benefits of receiving help. Beneficence at its core includes the highest desire of the caregiver to preserve life, to alleviate suffering, and to help the patient in a positive way. It is a principle that finds its expression in what many times is called *compassion*. Most physicians have practiced beneficence in the pursuit of their vocation in such a self-sacrificing way that their patients have come to think of them as a member of their own family. True love and trust have developed over many years of interaction and caring service, resulting in a strong human bond and emotional attachment between patient and physician. This desire of the physician to help and "do good" for the patient is a cornerstone of good medicine.

2. Nonmaleficence: the duty to "do no harm."

Hippocrates wrote, "I will use treatment to help the sick according to my ability and judgment, but never with a view to injury and wrongdoing. Neither will I administer a poison to anybody when asked to do so. . . . Into whatsoever house I enter, I will enter to help the sick, and I will abstain from all intentional wrong-doing and harm."[10] Ultimately, every physician and caregiver must come to terms with how treatment is affecting a patient and family and whether the risks and burdens outweigh the benefits of a specific treatment. Many medical interventions can cause harm in the long run. In any given situation to "do no harm" can lead to a variety of decisions.

For instance, in making a decision about Mildred's care in our earlier example, the ER physician and Bonnie had to evaluate the burden of keeping Mildred on life support and putting her through additional suffering when she would die regardless. And, second, they had to assess the benefits of moving Mildred to another hospital, where she would be away from her family and friends. In either of these two alternatives the principle of attempting to do no harm entered into the decision-making process.

3. Autonomy: personal freedom and responsibility.

Autonomy, or individual freedom of choice, is the principle that focuses on the promotion of personal responsibility for one's own life and actions. It has emerged as the most powerful principle in American bioethics, the basis of most regulation and the center of bioethics theory, and has become the default principle—the principle to be appealed to—when other principles conflict. Its place in medical decision making is described by one writer as follows:

> Autonomy refers to personal choice, control, and self-definition. Autonomy assumes the existence of individual values that do not need to be shared by others in order to be worthy of respect. In health care, patient autonomy is seen as the patient's right to receive accurate information about his or her health and treatment; to be fully informed not only about the physician's recommendations but also about alternative treatments that might preserve life, prevent disease, and relieve suffering; and to choose or to refuse any of those treatments. In addition, patient autonomy is served by permitting patients to choose others to hold and receive information and to make their decisions for them, whether physician, family member, or attorney-in-fact (as in the circumstance of granting durable power of attorney).[11]

Since autonomy has risen to such a prominent position in American law and federal regulation, it has raised several red flags in the eyes of those who know that responsibility to the *common* good, as represented in the principles of beneficence and justice, can be short-circuited by an overemphasis upon personal autonomy. Edmund Pelegrino calls the primacy of autonomy over the principle of beneficence "the most radical reorientation in the long history of the Hippocratic tradition."[12] Fox and Swazey summarize the ultimate effect this reliance upon autonomy has upon personal rights and religious commitments when they write:

> In the prevailing ethos of bioethics, the value of individualism is defined in such a way, and emphasized to such a degree, that it is virtually severed from social and religious values concerning relationships between

individuals; their responsibilities, commitments, and emotional bonds to one another; the significance of the groups and of the societal community to which they belong; and the deep inward as well as outward influence that these have on the individual and his or her sense of the moral.[13]

Autonomy is a principle that has several downsides, which ought to serve as a reminder to us that when it is invoked other significant principles *may* be being ignored.

4. Justice: fairness and equality.

Justice in medical decision making concerns what is fair and equitable among people, including the allocation of scarce resources. The principles of *distributive* justice or *comparative* justice emphasize that persons of society should share similarly in the benefits and burdens as available to members of society at large. For instance, should expensive blood products be used for elective surgery when shortages occur in life-threatening circumstances? Blood is a scarce resource that provides great benefit. An example of the burden associated with a scarce resource would be the price of forgoing elective surgery.

Several questions come to the forefront when the principle of justice is raised in medical ethics. Should strict equality of resources be maintained, even if no one receives enough to extend life? Should contributing members of society, or those statistically most likely to recover from an illness, receive all they need while others with a poorer prognosis receive little or none? If people can "pay the bill," should they be given first priority for scarce resources? Or should full treatment be provided for everyone, especially for those who are poor and unable to advocate for themselves? The principle of justice and questions such as these are applied in each hospital in a unique way. Where the emphasis is placed is a matter for ethical discussion. Other ethical principles related to justice, and which often are included on lists of important principles for organizational ethics, include the duty to tell the truth (veracity), the duty to protect privacy (confidentiality), and the duty to keep promises (fidelity).

Now that we have briefly examined these four common (and influential) medical ethics principles, we can move on to what is most important when dealing with principles and personal feelings in ethical dilemmas. That is, our own operational value system.

Discovering Your Operational Value System

Besides the four principles listed above, there is an almost infinite number of what can be called "ethical principles," or *values,* that guide our lives. They are different for each one of us. These can be thought about as core beliefs or personal philosophies that guide or motivate decisions in our lives. They define the things we treasure the most, and so provide a basis in our inner world for the subtle ranking of things we deeply want or desire in a way that elevates some values over others. Our values determine how we will behave in certain situations. These ethical values directly relate to beliefs concerning what is right and proper and good. Some of them for the Christian might be from the Bible. But some of them also stem from unique living experiences that form a part of our personal histories or our family traditions. Some of them are so deeply a part of our thinking that it is difficult to name them. They are *felt* or intuited, rather than *thought.* Each one of us has a unique mix of these values that define our "operational value system." A part of our own personal growth is to be able to verbalize what values or principles we hold significant.

Some questions that we can ask ourselves to help us in the process of understanding include the following: What makes my life worth living? What is the purpose of life? Why do illness and disease affect me? Is the afterlife important to me? What makes up my personal code of conduct? How do I keep myself healthy? Does God love me or care about what I'm experiencing? Does God bring healing, or does the body heal itself? Is there evil in the world? Are certain faith practices important to me? How we answer questions such as these speaks volumes regarding ultimate values that play a role in decision making and life choices.

Sometimes values are elicited through treatment choices given us by a doctor. For example, after being asked a question about having a living will, one patient stated, "I'd never want to be on a life-support machine." The values inherent in this statement can be illuminated by following up with the question "Why?" The patient might then answer, "Because I don't want to be a burden to my family." This statement might tell something about the value the patient places upon personal independence, *or* family financial security, *or* the perceived time constraints of other family members. Continued exploration could lead to the verbalization of important values that provide a framework for this person's treatment decisions, as well as give insight into their operational value system.

Our values often surface more readily when we are confronted by a situation that involves a child. For instance, I happened to be on duty in our hospital when a ten-year-old boy was injured in an automobile accident. After several hours of heart-wrenching waiting and diagnostic testing, the neurosurgeon determined that the boy had suffered a fatal head wound that resulted in swelling (or herniation) of the brain. Herniation occurs when the brain swells in the cranial enclosure and then is pressed down into the spinal column, damaging all motor and primary bodily function impulses, including breathing. It is a nonsurvivable condition. The boy was taken to the ICU on life support. Because he was otherwise healthy, the physician wanted to see him become an organ donor. The family was shocked and looked to me for advice.

If you were in the hospital when this incident happened, supporting a family that you had known for many years as Christian friends, what questions would be in your mind? How would you advise this family? As parents one of the first thoughts they would no doubt have is, "We want to protect our baby from harm." This is a primal parental function and role that is subtly at the basis of all our thinking. It is a "principle" that guides parental decision making. One ramification of this deep commitment might be the reaction against cutting, and thereby hurting, the child's body in the surgery that would be necessary to follow through with organ donation. Parents often decline organ donation for their children because of this very reason. The graphic mental pictures of what their child's body would have to endure is too much for them to bear in this awful moment of stress when they realize their child may die. They can even be educated in the need for organ donation and may perhaps be listed themselves as organ donors if they should die, but the thought of having their child go through that process is too difficult for them. They need to be counseled that their child is no longer conscious and feels no pain, as is the case in brain death.

Another possible reaction of the parents in this situation is to disbelieve that their child is really dead. Brain death is a hard concept to grasp when the body of your ten-year-old son, whom you have loved and raised since birth, is still breathing and has the skin tone and color of life. Although it is perhaps an educational issue or a time issue of just becoming more accustomed to the idea that the boy will not survive (in other words facing inevitable denial and coming to terms with the new reality), the thought of death having occurred while the heart is beating is difficult for us. In my mind it helps to tell myself that the injury is nonsurvivable and that there is no possibility of a brain transplant or a technique to save the brain after such a devastating injury. I can then accept that the person I have known is gone. Some people's values, however, would never accept this. The heart would have to stop before they would concede that death has taken place. The sanctity of human life as a value is a strong one, and any perceived decision to take organs or take a life prior to *heart* death would never set well. If that belief is where the parents landed, then organ donation would never take place in this instance. For *you* then, as an advisor and support for the family, the role would be to *hear* their concerns, to *educate* regarding the dynamics of brain death, and to *allow* their decision to be their decision. To directly take a stance against them would not be helpful or right. They are having to grieve the sudden death of their son. That is where your attention now needs to be directed.

Incidents like this one bring us to moments of decision in our own lives. When discussing this case with a pastor friend, and asking him if he would make the decision to donate his son's organs if he were in this position, he responded "I couldn't make that decision for him. I would probably *not* donate my son's organs if I didn't know how he felt." This pastor has two young sons whom he loves very much. In saying this, he is being guided by a principle of decision making that holds the right of *individual decision* as a high value. Even to the point of allowing his young children to decide organ donation for themselves. After our discussion he went home and asked his boys whether they wanted to be organ donors. They had both already been exposed to organ donation and its benefits in their third- and sixth-grade classes at school. Both of them set their father at ease by saying they would *want* to be organ donors. In the family discussion that followed, they expressed being motivated by the Christian value and desire to *save life* even in the sacrificing of one's own life. These young boys showed a wonderful Christian maturity in talking about this issue. In this pastoral family they all learned something about their own personal operational value systems.

Other Values and Ethics Principles

As I have said, there are a wide range of ethics principles that are person-specific. When principles such as beneficence, nonmaleficence, autonomy, and justice are proposed as *the* primary guiding principles with which we have to do, we can confidently respond that *personal* ethics principles are equally as authoritative in any decision-making situation. In order to get an idea of the types of values religious leaders have, I surveyed fifty-five diverse religious leaders in a local community. They were asked to name four ethical principles important to them in their faith beliefs, and other ethical or moral values shared by members of their faith community. In total, I collected a list of 400 values and principles.[14] The following examples will give an idea of the scope and variety of principles that can affect our decision making.

Given the context of medical ethics and the pastoral role of support and spiritual advocacy, the greatest number of values listed by these fifty-five clergy could be grouped in the *relational* category (133 responses). Values listed by them included: truthfulness, honesty, fairness, justice, respect, acceptance, trust, integrity, responsibility, confidentiality, faithfulness, community values, collaboration, and forgiveness, among others. It was interesting to me that values in this category were mentioned more than twice as frequently as values in the category of second-highest incidence. They rated higher than specifically theological values in the minds of these ministers.

Values clustered around the theme of "sanctity of life" were very prominent in the survey (fifty-eight responses). Some of the personal values listed by the pastors here included sanctity of life, beneficence, abortion is killing, life, and "try hard not to kill." It was clear to me that the value of life was recognized by the local ministers. In addition, other theological values (forty-seven responses) listed by them included the reality of absolute truth, prayer and listening to God, the sovereignty of God, belief in an afterlife, salvation as a value, God's grace, God's judgment, persons as created in the image of God, hope, faith, and divine healing. All of these were listed as values that the pastors would reflect upon during a critical decision-making time and that would influence how they made a decision.

"Freedom of choice" values were also very commonly held by these ministers (forty-two responses). Other ways they expressed this value included autonomy, following wishes of patient and family, individualism, tolerance, privacy, and individual dignity. "Love as a value" received many responses as well (forty responses). A wise pastor comes to realize very quickly that his or her congregation members have a variety of unique understandings and feelings. "Freedom of choice" values coupled with "love as a value" allow a pastoral advocate to freely support families according to their own needs and wishes. Many of the pastors additionally spoke of the "ministry of the Word" as they sought to be with families in difficult times of tragedy and illness.

So there are a variety of personal values and principles that act within us as our operational value system as we face medical decision making. The four common ethics principles of beneficence, nonmaleficence, autonomy, and justice are supplemented in every decision by a host of person-specific values and principles ranging from truthfulness (veracity), to faithfulness (fidelity), to respect, to the sanctity of life. But as we have also seen, in the midst of decision making, subtle values from past experience or family traditions also play a role.

In summary, there are a couple of very important aspects of this discussion of ethics principles that need to be reemphasized as we move on to look at ethical dilemmas in coming chapters. First, we need to have an awareness that a person's *operational value system* is more complicated than simply following biblical values. Hopefully, Christians will have the foundation of a biblical worldview as the basis for how they make decisions. But as previous examples have shown, even biblical Christians may approach medical decisions from differing perspectives. What is important is that each person be able to verbalize and have some awareness of why they hold the values they do. Our operational value systems stem not only from biblical principles but also from unique living experiences, our personal histories, and our family traditions. And as we converse and learn about another's value system, we need to come with a humble and teachable spirit so that trust and an open attitude in speaking of these very personal values can be assured. If we are to be a Christian support and advocate to those who need us, then we need to be able to hear what is important to *them* in a medical decision-making situation.

Second, as biblical Christians meeting life in the contemporary medical center, and invading (as it were) sometimes hostile territory, we need to be aware that *our* moral and personal values/principles are equally as important as beneficence, autonomy, justice, and nonmaleficence. Although these "Big Four" have influenced medical moral reflection and have played a role in the development of health-care ethics, in any ethical conflict in which *we* are involved as Christian advocates it is the patient's and family's ethical values and principles that are most important. Physicians and other medical personnel are bound by patient's rights legislation to offer care and medical treatment in keeping with the values and traditions of their patients and families. If those values can be verbalized and communicated to the medical providers, then medical decision making is made much easier.

So to better understand the workings of our operational value system and to provide some awareness of our role in advocacy we will next look at traumatic experiences and how these critical events from our personal histories affect how we will respond to new crisis experiences and to those families who ask us to be their advocates.

Notes

1. Stanley J. Grenz, *The Moral Quest* (Downers Grove, IL: InterVarsity Press, 1997), 23.

2. William S. Sahakian, *Systems of Ethics and Value Theory* (New York: Philosophical Library, 1963), 2–3.

3. "Hippocratic Oath" in *New Dictionary of Christian Ethics & Pastoral Theology*, ed. David John Atkinson, David Field, Arthur F. Holmes, Oliver O'Donovan (Leicester, UK: Universities and Colleges Christian Fellowhip, 1995), 442.

4. Patricia Flynn, "The Disciplinary Emergence of Bioethics and Bioethics Committees: Moral Ordering and Its Legitimation," *Sociological Focus* 24, no. 2 (1991): 147–48.

5. Judith Ross Wilson, *Handbook for Hospital Ethics Committees* (Chicago: American Hospital Association, 1986), 3.

6. Ibid., 3.

7. Ibid., 3.

8. This classic of medical ethics is still widely read and utilized by many in the teaching field; cf. Tom L. Beauchamp and James F. Childress, *Principles of Biomedical Ethics*, 5th ed. (New York: Oxford University Press, 2001).

9. Paul Root Wolpe, "The Triumph of Autonomy in American Bioethics; A Sociological View," in *Bioethics and Society*, ed. Raymond DeVries and Janardan Subedi (Upper Saddle River, NJ: Prentice-Hall, 1998), 41.

10. Jones, *Hippocrates,* 299–301.

11. Wilson, *Handbook for Hospital Ethics Committees*, 14.

12. Edmund D. Pelegrino, "The Relationship of Autonomy and Integrity in Medical Ethics," *Bulletin of PAHO* 24 (1990): 361.

13. Renée C. Fox and Judith P. Swazey, "Medical Morality Is Not Bioethics: Medical Ethics in China and the United States," *Perspectives in Biology and Medicine* 35 (1984): 358.

14. Kenneth P. Mottram, "Equipping Religious Leaders in Medical Ethics and Decision-Making Advocacy" (D. Min. diss., Golden Gate Baptist Theological Seminary, 2003), 99–104.

3

Advocacy, Trauma, and Personal Awareness

The best neighbors are ones that you can rely upon to help you when no one else is available. That is the kind of neighbor that I've always tried to be. I've wanted to get to know those who live around me, and then offer to water their plants or bring in their mail when they leave town. Sometimes the opportunity comes to really *be there* in a significant moment. Such was the case when my neighbor Joni got sick.

One evening, a young couple who knew I was employed at the hospital knocked on the door and expressed their concern about how Joni was acting. Sean and Kathryn kept in pretty good contact with Joni, who was a single woman and lived alone. But this evening she was unable to speak a full sentence when they telephoned her. They became concerned and knocked on her door, but she seemed incoherent and unable to unlock her door. Joni was a very accomplished professional person, and this was very much out of character for her. After several minutes of trying to get a response, they had decided to ask my opinion about what to do. They wondered if they should call the police or an ambulance to get Joni some help. After a few minutes of deliberation, we all decided that it would be better to err on the side of caution. We called the police, and in a few minutes a vehicle with flashing lights was pulling into the apartment parking lot. The police found Joni on the floor unable to move and barely conscious. It seemed that she was having some sort of convulsion. She was taken to the hospital in an ambulance. Sean, Kathryn, and I followed our friend to the ER by car. Kathryn had the phone number for Joni's mother, who lived several hundred miles away. She called her and let her know what was happening. She made the call from outside the hospital on her cell phone. Sean and I waited in the ER until Joni was admitted. It turned out that a slight metabolic imbalance had caused Joni's problems, and she was discharged the next day, thankful for the intervention by her friends. But it was Kathryn who caught my attention during this event and who raised my awareness again of some of the issues involved in hospital patient advocacy.

Kathryn was noticeably spending a lot of time *outside* the hospital building when Joni was being evaluated in the ER. I finally decided to ask her about it, and she quickly stated, "I just can't spend much time in hospitals. They make me sick. Ever since my mother died I have just been this way." Kathryn's mother had died from cancer four or five years before. I knew that it was a big loss for Kathryn and Sean and that they often had alluded to me what it was like for them to see her go downhill and finally die. I knew that they had a hard time even now watching movies where there was a protracted death scene, whether of a human being or an animal. A few days later I asked Kathryn about her experience that evening. She said that when she goes into a hospital she starts to get generally uncomfortable. Her stomach tightens, she gets a headache, and eventually feelings of nausea develop. She suspected that her blood pressure and pulse rate were elevated during those stressful hospital visits. Interestingly enough, this is *not* an unusual experience limited only to Kathryn or a few other grief-stricken daughters who have lost mothers. This experience is more widespread than we would expect. Many persons have continuing effects from past traumatic memories. In Kathryn's case the traumatic memories and resulting symptoms were triggered when she came near a hospital.

Personal experience as a hospital chaplain has opened my eyes to the variety of responses people have when they enter a medical setting. Because *I* always felt relaxed and "at home" when visiting patients in hospitals or nursing homes, even during the earliest years of ministry, I expected this to be the case for everyone. When I discovered that even some professional church leaders *actively avoid* the hospital and, if they do force themselves to go there, feel personally uncomfortable the entire time, I was amazed! The fact is that ministers too are individuals who have had a multiplicity of personal experiences that have affected them and that continue to play a role in their personalities and behaviors. Life experiences such as the death of a loved one in the hospital emergency room, or the loss of a mother to cancer in an oncology unit, or other traumatic losses that have left an indelible scar upon their lives continue to return as unpleasant flashbacks and other physiological symptoms each time a minister or other advocate enters the medical setting. The impact of such traumatic residual memories should not be underestimated.

Therese A. Rando, a leading voice in the current research linking posttraumatic stress reactions to the mourning of a significant loss, writes of the mental, emotional, spiritual, and physical effects that can occur when someone experiences traumatic events.[1] An individual so affected may be unaware of the source of such uncomfortable feelings when entering the hospital setting; the effect is to throw him or her off balance and derail an open understanding of the hospital visit. Self-education and self-awareness are effective means to combat this pitfall in being an effective advocate. Therefore, it is important to understand the dynamics of trauma and traumatic stress in order to bring some personal awareness of the blind spots *we* might succumb to as we seek to be advocates in decision-making situations.

Trauma and Its Effects

Lula M. Redmond was the first grief therapist to acknowledge that posttraumatic stress disorder (PTSD) is an expected outcome of the death of a loved one.[2] In fact, the loss of someone important to us is possibly the most traumatic crisis a person may experience in life. According to the American Psychiatric Association's *Desk Reference to the Diagnostic Criteria from DSM-IV-TR*, posttraumatic stress symptoms are prompted when a person "has been exposed to a traumatic event in which both of the following were present: (1) the person experienced, witnessed, or was confronted with an event or events that involved actual or threatened death or serious injury, or a threat to the physical integrity of self or others, and (2) the person's response involved intense fear, helplessness, or horror."[3] In other words, death, or being in the presence of death, is a stress-symptom prompter. The stress symptoms elicited may or may not be severe enough to meet the criteria of full-blown PTSD, but some of the symptoms are to be expected. In my experience of being with many families and friends as they have come to the hospital following the death of a loved one, the trauma cannot be minimized. We are shielded from death in our American culture, and when we finally are confronted by it our response is one of threat and fear. Some have called this the *shock effect* of death. Regarding this phenomenon Rando writes, "As coping abilities are completely overwhelmed the unanticipated loss leaves the survivor stunned, feeling out of control, bewildered, insecure, self-reproachful, and despairing."[4] In addition, the unanticipated physical symptoms of the sudden loss are particularly upsetting and combine with the emotional distress to overwhelm the person's ability to cope. What is it that happens to us to bring such a strong response?

Part of what happens concerns, first of all, our belief system and spirituality. When our lives are running smoothly and our minds are consumed by everyday issues of paying the bills, planning our next project on the job, or looking forward to the next vacation out of town, we hold to the assumptions that life is predictable, has a well-mannered pattern, and is somewhat under our control. Being confronted by death invades, upsets, and shatters those assumptions. When someone dies unexpectedly through accident or illness, the world as orderly and predictable is suddenly nothing of the kind. We find ourselves vulnerable, and we are faced with the fact of our own mortality. The resultant feelings of loss of control, defenselessness, and fear bring us to a new place in our belief system. We question God's presence in what happened. The question is not only "Why did this happen?" but also "Will God let this happen to me?" We might feel a profound loss of personal security in God and confidence that God will watch over us.

These feelings happen quickly and sometimes are not even verbalized by those experiencing them, but their effects are evident. We're confused and suddenly bombarded with a variety of feelings: anger, guilt, helplessness, regret, ambivalence, anxiety, etc. Do we feel that God is with us? Do we know his peace that passes all understanding? Do we place the events in God's hands and rest in the knowledge that his purposes will be accomplished? Sometimes yes and sometimes no. Regardless, the death hits us very hard and brings questions of faith and assumptions about normal life to the forefront of our thinking.

A second troubling aspect of a death occurs when we actually see the dead body. Unless we're in a profession where we're exposed to death regularly, the experience of being in the presence of a lifeless body is unforgettable. Not only do we not forget it, every detail of what we saw, heard, smelled, touched, or tasted during that time remains with us, stored in memory. When the normal coping mechanisms we utilize to deal with life's disappointments or tragedies are overwhelmed, such as in the sudden loss of someone very important to us, and we have to face something very frightening and are helpless to change the outcome, all of our senses experience hyperarousal and record the data being inputted with great detail in a process called *sensory brain imprinting*. In effect, the trauma of being with the body results in the overload of all five physical senses and in the creation of a memory that is very vivid and real. From this we can experience posttraumatic flashbacks of what was recorded. This is a very normal, common, and predictable experience that affects all human beings when subjected to the right conditions.

According to *DSM-IV-TR* some of the stress reactions that can result from such a traumatic experience include: sudden visual flashbacks that enter our awareness during regular day activities, dream flashbacks at night, feelings that the traumatic event is recurring (a sense of reliving the event), intense distress at exposure to similar circumstances (e.g., visiting the hospital again), and persistent avoidance of the stimuli associated with the trauma (i.e., avoidance of thoughts, feelings, conversations, activities, places, or people that bring back the memory).[5] The flashbacks are not always visual but can involve one or all of the five senses.

I have been very aware of this phenomenon as I have taken families back into the ER trauma room to view the body of someone they love. One needs to be sensitive to the fact that they will remember every detail of the experience and that many of the details will be traumatic to them. I remember one family situation in which an adult son was killed in a work-related accident. When he was brought to the ER a wide variety of life-saving measures were used to attempt to revive him. As a result he was bloated from fluid being pumped into his veins, he was intubated (the breathing tube with its attendant apparatus is always intrusive-looking and frightening), the scent of blood and other bodily fluids was evident, and his color was gray-blue. He still had some blood visibly seeping from his nose and ears. These are not the type of lasting memories families usually desire to have of a son. I tried to prepare them by describing what they would see. If, as an advocate, you suspect possible injuries to the patient that might be traumatic for the family, I recommend you view the body before the family does to help give your first impressions to the family as a means of minimizing the possible shock to them. In this case the four family members decided to go together to see the son. The mother cried out immediately upon entering the trauma room and hugged her son, kissing his forehead and stroking his blood-soaked hair. She sobbed for nearly ten minutes with her head on his chest. The others—which included the father, an uncle, and a sister—all stood by crying and hugging one another. There is no doubt in my mind that the mother was on sensory overload. This was a death that came too soon and was a shocking reminder to her of the frailty of life. When she was that close to her dead son, she could not only *see* his injuries (seeping blood), but also *smell* his body, *hear* the ER personnel talking in the distance about their latest ski trip (a negative memory for a grieving mother), *taste* the fluids on the skin and clothing of the son, and *feel* the swollenness of his body and the stillness of death. The totality of her sensory experience was being imprinted on her brain at that moment and would be remembered for years to come as one of the most terrible experiences of her life. Eventually they asked me to pray for their son, and I gathered all of them around him, holding hands, as we gave him back to God. As the family left, I wondered how the mother's life would be affected by the trauma she experienced that day. There are no words to soothe the loss and hurt. But to affirm and know that God loved the son and took care of him in this accident is an important recognition of faith and needs to be verbalized and brought to the minds of the family.

I personally experienced a posttraumatic stress flashback two days after I attended a trauma code in which a burn victim was brought to our ER. The accident happened as this man was reloading shells of ammunition in his basement while smoking a cigarette. The gunpowder ignited and exploded, setting the whole house aflame. The man was able to find his way out, but he was badly burned over 60 percent of his body. I was very proud of our team of RNs in the ER as they worked to save this man whose wounds were nearly fatal and who reeked of burnt flesh and hair. One RN was particularly close to him for nearly an hour, attempting to maintain an airway and keep instruments functioning. The smell was horrendous and had pervaded the ER. I got close enough to the patient to at least tell him that his family was on the way and that I was praying for him. In a few hours he was flown to a burn center in a neighboring state. I was approached the next day by the RN who had spent so much time helping the patient. He related that he had been unable to sleep the night before because of his experience and was worried about continued flashbacks. I listened as he "self-debriefed" the experience. Because he was a seasoned ER nurse, he knew that talking about the incident and relating as many details as possible would help him to get over it.

Surprisingly, the next morning as I drove into the ER parking lot, I could distinctly smell the stench of burning flesh and hair that had been so prominent two days ago. It was that unmistakable smell that had made me recoil and think twice about entering the trauma room to talk to the burned patient. I looked down at my clothing, wondering if I was wearing the same shirt or pants that I had worn two days ago, but the clothing was all different. It entered my mind that some of the smell could have collected on my shoes, but why did I smell it only when driving into the ER parking area? Then I realized that this was an olfactory hallucination—a flashback of a smell that had been imprinted in my memory—as real as if I were in that same trauma room right next to that burned patient. It was a frightening experience for me to realize that I was susceptible to hallucinations that seemed so real, yet such reactions are a common and normal human experience that we all should know can affect us when we are exposed to traumatic events or situations.

Other Factors That Lead to Trauma

Trauma can be defined as "an emotional state of discomfort and stress resulting from memories of an extraordinary, catastrophic experience which shattered the survivor's sense of invulnerability to harm."[6] Although most deaths are subjectively and *internally* traumatic, some types of deaths should raise additional red flags because of the *outward* circumstances of the death. Rando lists five factors that make a specific death objectively traumatic and that, for us, serve to bring further understanding in our attempt to anticipate a possible traumatic response.[7]

1. Any sudden, unanticipated death

An unanticipated death leaves a person stunned and numb, wondering how and why something so terrible could have happened. The full extent of the loss certainly cannot be absorbed in a short time. A gradual process is needed to help the surviving family and friends come to grips with the new information. Close family are often struck by the fact that there was no chance to say good-bye. They remember the last time they spoke to the person now gone and are angry that they did not know it would be the last time they would have a chance to converse. Sometimes a family member becomes hysterical.

I remember a particularly terrible accident in which a middle-aged father was crushed under a piece of heavy equipment on the work site. He was brought to our hospital, and although emergency surgery was attempted, he didn't survive the first thirty minutes. I was in the family support room when his wife, Heidi, and her brother Bill came through the door. She had received a phone call from her husband's supervisor that her husband had been critically injured in an industrial accident. Heidi was particularly upset and shaking as she asked, "Do you know anything yet?" It is usually the place of the physician to explain what is happening with the patient, and in the case of a death, to break the news to the family. Although I knew her husband was already dead, I went quickly to get the ER doctor to speak to Heidi and inform her of her husband's passing. As he entered the room, the look on his face alone sent Heidi into hysterics. She began wailing, tears streaming down her face. Heidi didn't hear a word of the doctor's caring and compassionate efforts to explain. All she knew was that her husband was dead. The doctor's face reflected his concern and need of help even before he said the words: "I don't know what to do. She's all yours."

When Heidi saw the doctor leaving the room she got up from her seat, muscles tense and fists clenched, and went after him as if to attack him. The physician restrained her, putting his arms around her and holding her back. She was screaming, "This is unfair! What has happened to my husband? Where is he? What have you done with him?" I went to them and put my arms around them both, upon which I was promptly rewarded with a quick elbow to the stomach from Heidi. The doctor and I both circled the small room with Heidi dragging us, screaming, fighting, and crying for what seemed an eternity. We did what we could to try to calm her down. Finally she collapsed on the floor sobbing, "I didn't get a chance to say good-bye to him. I didn't get a chance to kiss him good-bye." It turned out that he had left the house with his kids to drop them off at school while she was still taking her morning shower. That was the last morning he was to live. Heidi would never see her husband again.

In this sudden death situation Heidi experienced many of the factors that make grieving more intense for loved ones who have to deal with a sudden loss. She had to process the fact that she would not see her husband again. In this instance she was not allowed into the postsurgery room because of the bodily deformation experienced from the accident and from the surgery. I don't know if she was even able to view the body at the funeral home, but probably not. The reality of death is only made more difficult to accept when the body cannot be seen. Heidi also had no chance to say goodbye, which often leads to a variety of grief issues or other regrets that could follow her for years to come. She also exhibited the very intense emotional reaction that sudden death often precipitates. She was probably a high-strung person, anyway—definitely demonstrative with her emotions—but she still predictably followed the pattern of anger, helplessness, confusion, and disorganization, along with strong needs to determine blame and affix responsibility for the death. One can only imagine what kinds of permanent feelings Heidi would take from this horrible experience and what would follow her through the years whenever she might have the occasion to enter a hospital again.

2. A violent death or any death where the body is physically marred or grotesque

After a sudden, unanticipated death, the second type of objectively traumatic death is one that is violent or in which the body is physically marred. Deaths involving violence, or particularly devastating fatal means, where the body is mutilated and perhaps left in a grotesque fashion, prompt in the mourners the most primitive of fears and the most basic death anxieties. Survivors in such situations often find themselves focusing on what the loved one *felt* or experienced at the time of death. This posttraumatic *imagery* can be particularly overwhelming as loved ones' imaginations attempt to reconstruct what the deceased went through at the time of death and the helplessness *they* feel at not being able to alleviate that suffering. Since persons who die in these situations usually also fit into the category of sudden death, the same processing that Heidi experienced would be typical in a violent death as well. Although Heidi didn't verbalize concerns about what her husband felt at the time of his death that day at the hospital, I suspect it crossed her mind many times later when she was thinking about his accident.

3. Any random death or one that was preventable

Surviving family and friends in preventable deaths cannot help but view such tragedies as something that did not have to occur. The death could have been avoided. Often workplace deaths fall into this category. Safety is normally priority number one on the job, which raises the anger of grieving families when accidents happen. The perception of preventability leads survivors to search for a cause or reason for the death and to seek punishment for negligence.

Although blame is often placed at the feet of some person, in many instances terrible accidents are just that—terrible accidents. Accidents in life bring out feelings of unfairness and injustice. Emotions are intensified, and a searching process to discover meaning in the loss usually follows.

Rando is particularly insightful in discussing the inner processing of those who lose a significant person in a truly random death:

> Truly random events are especially terrifying because they are unpredictable and therefore uncontrollable: Individuals cannot protect themselves from them. Therefore, a common tendency on the parts of mourners and those who have been victimized by random events is to assume blame for

them. It is relatively easier to cope with an event's being one's own responsibility—and thus potentially being within one's own control—than it is to contend with the fact that it was a genuinely random event. The assumption of blame is the price to be paid to maintain the needed perception that the world is not random and unpredictable, but orderly and dependable. This is similar to the psychological dynamics behind the phenomenon of "blaming the victim." In both cases, there is an attempt to take the event out of the realm of a random occurrence against which one cannot protect oneself and make it manageable by identifying elements the survivor can control or avoid in the future to forestall a recurrence.[8]

Someone once said that it is easy to "call foul" on another person but difficult to recognize one's own indiscretions. And in a case where something as subtle as *assuming* blame for an event outside of one's own ability to influence takes hold of us, we should not expect or pretend to recognize all the dynamics at play within our own internal workings. But we can certainly become more self-aware. In this instance, a person who is dealing with a random death and attempting to make sense of it would no doubt undergo a radical shift in worldview or personal understanding of the makeup of life events in general. And if put into a decision-making position regarding health care that might involve facing death or end-of-life issues (or if advocating for someone in that position), a person so affected would seek to maintain personal control and would move toward decisions that would protect life at all costs. And this, even if the best of medical science says to let go and let life processes take their natural course. We are always affected in subtle ways by past experiences that have made an impact on our lives.

4. Multiple deaths

A fourth objectively traumatic type of death occurs when multiple deaths happen concurrently. Any time two or more loved ones are lost in a single event or closely related events, a multiple-death grief situation is operative. Examples of how this might happen include: a natural catastrophe (hurricane, earthquake, tornado, fire, etc.), a murder-suicide, an automobile accident, an airline accident, or some other unforeseen accident. These situations always bring difficulties in coping for the survivors, and difficulties for spiritual-support persons as well. However, from my experience I think people are also drastically affected when two or more persons close to them are lost in a relatively short period of time, for instance, during the same calendar year. I don't know how many times I have spoken to family members who have lost a mother, a sister, an uncle, and a good friend all within the same year and had them express how difficult it has been to cope with the multiple losses. They would say, "This year has been just awful." In such cases people can experience what some therapists have called *bereavement overload*. We become overwhelmed with the size of our personal loss, and it makes us numb and moves our minds to grief, reflection, and reprioritization of what is important in life. If all of the persons lost through death have been significant in our lives, then we have complicated grief cycles in which we cannot adequately grieve for person A because the deaths of persons B and C have entered our life experience. And we cannot even grieve adequately for persons B and C because we are still affected by the loss of person A. The bereavement period becomes longer, and our lives are affected throughout that grieving time period.

Once again, if we are then thrust into a life-or-death decision-making position regarding someone's health during this time of bereavement overload, we will inevitably seek to make decisions to save life and protect ourselves from additional grief or pain. It is a common occurrence in hospitals around the country that people are not allowed to die with dignity because of the pain already being suffered by well-meaning family members who cannot see it in their hearts to lose another loved one.

5. A personal encounter with death or the body

A final circumstance that makes a specific death traumatic is when there is a personal encounter with the body that is outside of one's normal experience and threatens one's understanding of life and what is normal about the world. Finding a family member who has completed suicide is a terrible shock. Similarly, having to identify the body of a child, or a burn victim, or a drowning victim are all traumatic events that commonly lead to posttraumatic stress reactions involving all five senses and traumatic brain imprinting leading to cognitive, physiological, and emotional stress reactions. Personal counseling is often needed after a traumatic experience such as these.

I have frequently spoken to patients who have been in automobile accidents in which a fatality occurred. Sometimes the driver survives and is confronted with the mutilated body of a passenger who is still breathing after the accident but who dies while the driver is trapped in the vehicle. I remember one husband who lost his wife in such a circumstance. I sat in the hospital room next to his bed and let him tell the story of his final minutes with his wife and all of the detail that he remembered about her death. Such experiences can be reckoned as the worst memories that one ever has to hold.

Summary

Our personal histories and the ramifications that continue to affect us from events that have impacted our lives play a key role in our operational value system. The lasting effects of personal trauma experiences and the deaths of significant persons can't help but influence how we respond in medical decision-making situations in the here and now. And just as Kathryn found being in the hospital surroundings difficult, we too might exhibit avoidance behavior that would keep us from being effective in an advocacy role. What we seek is personal awareness of our own feelings and values and *why* we feel the way we do. If we are going to be effective advocates and compassionate Christian support persons for others who have to face difficult dilemmas and medical decision-making choices, then we need to have a good idea of the ways our own histories have come to be and be able to objectively set them aside in order to respond to the needs of those we are sincerely seeking to support. It is a daunting task, but one that pays wonderful rewards as we are able to be instruments of God's blessing in the lives of those who are important to us.

Notes

1. Therese A. Rando, *Treatment of Complicated Mourning* (Champaign, IL: Research Press, 1993).

2. Lula M. Redmond, *Surviving: When Someone You Love Was Murdered* (Clearwater, FL: Psychological Consultation and Education Services, 1989).

3. American Psychiatric Association, *Desk Reference to the Diagnostic Criteria from DSM-IV-TR* (Washington, DC: American Psychiatric Association, 2000).

4. Therese A. Rando, "Complications in Mourning Traumatic Death," in *Living with Grief after Sudden Loss*, ed. Kenneth J. Doka (Washington, DC: Hospice Foundation of America, 1996), 145.

5. American Psychiatric Association, *Desk Reference to the Diagnostic Criteria*, 218–22.

6. C. R. Figley, "Role of the Family: Both Haven and Headache," in *Role Stressors and Supports for Emergency Workers*, ed. M. Lystad (Washington, DC: DHHS Publication no. (ADM) 85-1408, 1985), xviii.

7. Rando, "Complications in Mourning Traumatic Death," 145–52.

8. Ibid., 149.

4

A Biblical Look at Ethics and Advocacy

Many of the people I encounter confess that they have been in situations that caused them to doubt a choice they had to make in a matter of conscience. One divorced woman related that she felt she could have done more to save her marriage, but that she knew of troubles in her life that could be traced to her unsatisfying marriage relationship and so took actions that eventually led to the breakup. She confessed, "Did I do the right thing? I'm not sure." A man from the Northwest said, "I lied to human services so I could feed my children, because the system is set against a white male who 'should' be able to work." A physician expressed guilt for referring a patient within the managed care system when a surgical specialist in a teaching hospital could possibly have offered better answers for the man's critical disease. In our complicated twenty-first-century world there are often situations that fall into the gray area between clearly right and clearly wrong, and unfortunately many of our friends and family struggle with these questions on their own, with no independent moral standard with which to measure themselves. We live in a culture typified by an ethical vacuum. People often make up their own truth as the circumstances dictate. Pragmatism is a common way of describing this life-philosophy characteristic of many of the individuals we meet in our day-to-day interactions. In *pragmatic theory* truth is "what works."[1] People can in effect make up their own truth to fit whatever problem is confronting them. However, since "what works" is a subjective determination and person-specific in scope, pragmatism is merely a form of relativism. As the philosophers Peter Kreeft and Ronald Tacelli note, G. E. Moore brought into focus the problem with pragmatic theory and helps us to see the faulty reasoning behind it:

> G. E. Moore proved (in his essay "William James's Pragmatism") that the pragmatic theory of truth is based on a linguistic confusion. There is a perfectly good word in the language for "what works." That word is "efficient" or "effective" or "practical." If we reduce truth to "what works," we lose a different, distinctive, independent meaning of truth as "saying what is." Moore shows quite simply and conclusively that truth cannot mean "what works" or "what is practical," because what is true is not always practical (e.g., death) and what is practical is not always true (e.g., a "successful" lie).[2]

In contrast to this common but abject philosophy of pragmatism, the Christian's belief is that God has spoken to us in a "revelational" way and disclosed Truth that is true and reflective of the realities we find in life. Christians look to a book, the Bible, for objective truth providing an independent source of guidance in ethical matters.

Accordingly, Christians can be characterized as "people of the Book." Stanley Grenz writes, "This description is appropriate in that we acknowledge the Bible as embodying divine revelation and for this reason continually look to the scriptures for instruction as to what we should believe and what we should do. We desire to be informed by the Bible so that we might live faithfully before God as followers of Jesus Christ."[3] We hold scripture to be our word from God and inspired by the Holy Spirit, sensing that truth breathes through its pages. In 2 Timothy 3:16–17 we are reminded that "all Scripture is God-breathed and is useful for teaching, rebuking, correcting and training in righteousness, so that the man of God may be thoroughly equipped for every good work." The psalmist adds additional weight to this Christian doctrine of inspiration and authority by writing, "As for God, his way is perfect; the word of the LORD is flawless. He is a shield for all who take refuge in him" (Ps. 18:30). And again in Psalm 19:7, "The law of the LORD is perfect, reviving the soul. The statutes of the LORD are trustworthy, making wise the simple." Christians from every nation and culture of our world have found the Bible to be a sure voice in speaking truth about human experience and the spiritual realities that are part of life. It is a special gift from God to his people and a wondrous strength for us during times of questioning as well as when we need guidance in decision making.

There are three foundational points that I feel need to be made as Christians seek a biblical theology for engaging in advocacy in decision making. Of course, an exhaustive biblical theology of medical ethics would be more far-reaching. But here at least the foundation needs to be laid for reflective action as we seek to do our part as God's instruments in attempting to "carry each other's burdens" (Gal. 6:2).

First, it is important to set the task of doing medical ethics in its Christian context as stemming from the revealed character of God. God has revealed himself in history through mighty acts and interventions in the lives of people. God has told us his name. He has specific attributes that describe his Person. Second, the value of human beings as created in the image of God needs to be addressed. Because we are created in God's image, we have inestimable value and have a God-given right to be treated with personal dignity and respect. Third, a biblical basis for Christian ethical advocacy is important, and the apostle Paul left us a wonderful record of an ethical dilemma and an example of advocacy described in his letter to Philemon. Paul modeled a human ethic informed by concern for persons who were his "children" in the faith. This short letter provides a good look at advocacy in a New Testament context.

The Ethical Task Stems from the Revealed Character of God

According to the Bible, God chose certain persons to be his instruments in bringing the wider human family to an understanding of his nature. Moses was one such person (Exod. 2). He was a man of Hebrew origin who lived as a minority in the highly developed culture of Egypt. Found as an infant by Pharaoh's daughter in the Nile River, he was saved from certain death and then was raised as Egyptian royalty in Pharaoh's household, receiving an education of the upper class. As an adult he was forced into exile when he murdered an Egyptian citizen who was mistreating a Hebrew slave. One day as he was tending the flock of Jethro, his father-in-law, in the region of Midian, he observed a bush that was on fire but did not burn up. The abnormality of the event and Moses's reaction are stated in Exodus 3:3. "So Moses thought, 'I will go over and see this strange sight—why the bush does not burn up.'" Moses is here described as being drawn to an unusual occurrence that did not fit his understanding of the events of nature—a bush that did not succumb to fire. When he approached the bush a voice called to him "from within the bush," identifying Moses by name and saying "I am the God of your father, the God of Abraham, the God of Isaac and the God of Jacob" (Exod. 3:4–6). Moses responded as any human being would respond to such an experience, that is, with fear and an attempt to hide. The irrational and unexplainable (according to the laws of nature) experience of the bush and the Voice are clearly relayed through the written account.

The drama of God's call to Moses to be an instrument of liberation for his oppressed Hebrew people is exciting reading and, when carried to fruition by Moses's acceptance of God's call, is the beginning of a whole set of unusual occurrences and miracles (God's intervention in history) that eventually changed the culture of two nations, that of the Egyptians and that of the Hebrews. The Jewish Seder celebrated yearly to this day (Exod. 12) is a testimony to the historicity and cultural impact of this event. The essence of Judeo-Christian belief is that God has spoken through *revelatory history*. The writer of 2 Peter summarized the Christian view of revelation and the unique nature of God speaking *through* persons in these words: "We did not follow cleverly invented stories when we told you about the power and coming of our Lord Jesus Christ, but we were eyewitnesses of his majesty. . . . Above all, you must understand that no prophecy of Scripture came about by the prophet's own interpretation. For prophecy never had its origin in the will of man, but men spoke from God as they were carried along by the Holy Spirit" (2 Pet. 1:16, 20–21).

Old Testament ethicist Christopher Wright stresses the differences between pragmatism and history as competing foundations for ethics in these words: "God was believed to have acted, and to be continuously active, in history; therefore events and sequences of events took on moral significance. Without this conviction of God's active involvement and interest in affairs, ethics becomes pragmatic and even dispensable. For who cares? But because it was such a live conviction in Israel, there developed a whole genre of literature which we tend, by familiarity, to take for granted—namely prophetic historical narrative."[4] It is this prophetic historical narrative that includes not only the Ten Commandments (the foundational human ethic, cf. Exod. 20), but also the writings of Amos, Micah, Isaiah, Jeremiah, et al., culminating in the life and teachings of Jesus of Nazareth.

Douglas Groothuis has pointed to the recent philosophical trend of the postmodern movement and its belief that "there is no moral reality to be known apart from the cultures that create them" and the writings of Richard Rorty, Michel Foucault, and Jean-François Lyotard, who believe that "we are historically conditioned 'all the way down'" as standing against the Christian understanding of revelatory truth.[5] The recent bioethical approaches of Glenn McGee,[6] Joseph Fins, and others who follow the pragmatic model of John Dewey and James H. Tufts[7] and opt for a naturalistic bioethics have been embraced by many contemporary ethicists and also fall into the postmodern mold. Grenz has summarized the effect this has had from a Christian perspective:

> Postmodernism has tossed aside objective truth, at least as it has classically been understood. Foucault, Derrida, and Rorty stand against what has for centuries been the reigning epistomological principle—the correspondence theory of truth (the belief that truth consists of the correspondence of propositions with the world "out there"). This rejection of the correspondence theory not only leads to a skepticism that undercuts the concept of objective truth in general; it also undermines Christian claims that our doctrinal formulations state objective truth.[8]

But the global community *is* joined together by a single objective manifestation of ultimate truth—God's revelation through the Jewish people—that encompasses all people groups and all times.[9] In contrast, then, to the naturalism of the pragmatists and the skepticism of the postmoderns, Christians have discovered a world loved by a transcendent God who speaks to persons and reveals truth in miraculous ways, giving an assurance to events of history, offering a view of truth that is objective, while taking seriously the experiences of spirituality among global people groups.

So the substance and content of Christian ethical behavior stems from nothing less than the revealed character of God. We are to act as God has modeled in his dealings with us in history. The clearest presentation of this principle is found in Leviticus: "Be holy because I, the LORD your God, am holy" (19:2). Christopher Wright defines "holiness" as a biblical concept:

> We are inclined to think of "holiness" as a matter of personal piety or, in Old Testament terms, of ritual cleanliness, proper sacrifices, clean and unclean foods, and the like. But the rest of Leviticus 19 shows us that the kind of holiness which reflects God's own holiness is thoroughly practical. It includes generosity to the poor at harvest time, justice for workers,

integrity in judicial processes, considerate behaviour to other people, equality before the law for immigrants, honest trading and other very "earthy" social matters. And all through the chapters runs the refrain: "I am the Lord," as if to say, "This is what I require of you because it is what I myself would do."[10]

Throughout the Old Testament, beginning with the Torah, imitation of the Lord is proposed as the human ethical standard.

This focus is likewise found in the teachings of Jesus Christ in the New Testament. Jesus embraced the Old Testament standard categorically: "Do not think that I have come to abolish the Law or the Prophets . . . until heaven and earth disappear, not the smallest letter, not the least stroke of a pen, will by any means disappear from the Law . . ." (Matt. 5:17–18). Then Jesus's own words exhort people to model their lives after the revealed character of God: "Be perfect, therefore, as your heavenly Father is perfect" (Matt. 5:48). However, Jesus also spoke with the authority of God the Father in setting out ethics for the kingdom of God. Mark 1:22 notes, "The people were amazed at his teaching, because he taught them as one who had authority, not as the teachers of the law." Concerning Jesus's authority, A. D. Verhey writes: "Here was not simply a pious interpreter of the law but one who announced God's coming sovereignty and made known God's sovereign will." Verhey sees the ethics Jesus embraced as characterized by servanthood, truthfulness, inward purity as opposed to outward law-keeping, and sacrificial love.[11] Certainly the uniqueness of Jesus Christ is found in the loving laying-down of his life as an act of obedience to God's purposes and in love of others. Jesus models the character of God as represented not through fear and the strength of coercion, but through lovingkindness and self-sacrifice for his people.

Therefore, from Moses and the receiving of the Ten Commandments, through Old Testament history and the revelatory narratives of the Prophets, and continuing into the New Testament and Jesus's ethic of love and giving of self for others, Christians have a sure word of truth and an inspiring testimony forming a basis for ethical reflection, all centered upon God's revealed character and our imitation of that character. This basis for a manifestation of Christian ethics is in opposition to the postmodern attack on truth and its emphasis upon diversity and cultural specificity.

Christian ethicist Tristram Engelhardt locates the theological foundation for bioethics in the living of a life in relationship to God. It involves turning from oneself *to God* and learning his ways. He writes,

"Christian bioethics is not merely an academic field over against the everyday fabric of life. If it succeeds truly in being a Christian bioethics, it is a Christian way of living, experiencing, and engaging in sexuality, reproduction, suffering, disease, disability, health care, and dying. It is a living response to all the challenges that frame bioethics."[12] For the Christian this foundation for ethics, which stems ultimately from the character of a holy God, offers the only compelling and intellectually viable approach to the current ethical task. An ethics resting upon revealed truth that has been handed down through millennia provides a surer foundation for decision making than do the variety of pragmatic and postmodern alternatives.

Human Beings Are Created in the Image of God

There are many ways to look at human beings in our society. Sigmund Freud impacted human studies in many disciplines when he postulated that humans were, in effect, biological machines who responded in predictable ways based upon biological drives, especially sexuality.[13] Again, some theorists today would emphasize the fact that human beings can be understood through physiology. B. F. Skinner, founder of behavioral psychology, saw humans as sophisticated animals that respond to positive or negative reinforcement in habitual patterns.[14] To Skinner, human beings are trainable. Adherents to his view would emphasize that greater society can be affected for the good through appropriate manipulation of the human animal. The Bible, on the other hand, states that human beings were created by the Lord God in a unique way and with distinctive characteristics. In contrast to Freud, Skinner, or other theorists of humanity, the Bible states that "God created man in his own image" (Gen. 1:27), thereby setting humanity apart from merely physiological, psychological, or other determinative theories and granting instead tremendous value and dignity. This value is ultimately imparted solely by the Creator God. In addressing this *theological* approach to value as opposed to the *anthropocentric* approach, Grenz writes:

> The declaration "God is Creator" provides the ultimate answer to the ethical question of value . . . philosophical ethics is concerned with what humans ought to value and what forms the basis for value judgments. The answers philosophers generally offer indicate the basically anthropocentric character of the philosophical approach. In the end the final

court of appeal can only be the human person and human conceptions of the good life. Humans value whatever they perceive contributes to that life. To acknowledge God as Creator, however, is to raise the discussion to the theocentric level and offer a theological foundation for value. The Christian ethic approaches questions of value from the scriptural account of the divine Valuer. All value is ultimately determined solely by the Creator God of the biblical narrative. As the one who values truly, God is the standard for value, and this God calls us to value after the manner our Creator values.[15]

It is this emphasis upon the value God places on human beings that is crucial for Christians who desire to follow a revelational approach to medical ethics and who seek a foundation for pastoral advocacy in medical decision making. And there are several aspects of the meaning of the "image of God" and its effect upon an understanding of the value of a human being that we will now consider.

First of all, there is a foundation for human *spirituality* in the fact that Man[16] was created in the image of God. Although Christians are more comfortable describing our dealings with God in terms of a *relationship* and not as *religion,* in the medical setting *spirituality* is viewed as the word of choice when describing personal faith commitments or religious traditions. In keeping with this medical preference, I believe that spirituality was bestowed in God's creative act and is a natural part of being in the image of God. In fact, spirituality is a way to speak of human relationship with God. Walter Brueggemann speaks of the special relationship evident in the act of creation when he writes, "It is important that of all the creatures of God's eight creative acts, God speaks directly only to human creatures. The others have no speech directed toward them at all. By contrast, in 1:28, God speaks to *the human creatures,* and in verse 29, he twice addresses them directly, 'you.' This creature has a different, intimate relation with the creator."[17] J. I. Packer also stresses this speaking of the Creator to Man as the beginning of a spiritual relationship: "Here God is addressing man directly; thus fellowship between God and man is inaugurated."[18] Karl Barth and Emil Brunner additionally develop this relational perspective of the *imago Dei* and its significance to the understanding of our value as human beings.[19] Through this spiritual aspect of creation, then, everyone possesses the potential for communion with God, and people will, no doubt, experience feelings of detachment or incompleteness until they come to grips with this part of their human makeup. All human beings have a spirituality that they must learn to identify and embrace as part of human living.

A second and equally significant aspect of the "image of God" concerns the sacred nature of Man. The image of God in scripture seems to be a universal human characteristic, since each one of us, no matter our racial or cultural background, has been created by the same God. Furthermore, the sanctity of human life is fundamentally grounded in this universal image of God in human beings. Over the centuries theologians have postulated various ideas concerning the meaning and nature of the *imago Dei* and what human characteristics exactly represent its presence, including the notion of intellectual capacity, or rational thought, or emotion and will, or dominion over creation, or sexuality as male and female, or moral reasoning, or the capacity to know God. The exact nature of the image of God within us is a mystery that has captured the imagination of theologians from the earliest years of church history. Recently, ethicists Scott Rae and Paul Cox have proposed a *substantive* understanding that suggests that the "image" is something inherent in the human makeup and *not* something merely possessed. They write, "The creation account makes it clear that the image of God is not something that human beings possess, but rather something they are. It is a constitutive element of being human, something that we are made in."[20] And again, "The image of God is not a capacity we possess or lose, but rather a part of our essence."[21] This is an attractive notion for several reasons, but especially as Christians consider the human value of embryos and fetuses. If embryos and fetuses carry the complete essence of the image of God, then they must be held as sacred and protected in medical decision making as full human beings.

Rae and Cox argue that scripture indicates a "continuity of identity" from the smallest human being at conception onward through life maturity. David in Psalm 139 writes, "For you created my inmost being; you knit me together in my mother's womb. I praise you because I am fearfully and wonderfully made; your works are wonderful, I know that full well" (vv.13–14). In verse 16 David describes himself as an "unformed body," translated by Brown, Driver, and Briggs as "embryo."[22] Rae and Cox summarize the significance of David's words by writing:

> David sees the person who gives thanks and praise to God in verses 13–16 as the same person who was skillfully "woven together" in the womb and is known by God inside and out in verses 1–6. In other words, there is continuity of personal identity from the earliest point of development to a mature adult. That is the significance of Psalm 139 to the discussion of the nature of the human person. It is not solely that God

painstakingly and intricately created David in the womb, but also that the person who was being created in the womb is the same person who is writing the psalm. . . . Thus, given the continuity of personal identity, it is not unreasonable to suggest that the divine image is present from the earliest points of embryonic life.[23]

Theologian Millard Erickson also sees the "image" in terms of essence:

> The image is something in the very nature of man, in the way in which he was made. It refers to something man *is* rather than something he *has* or *does*. By virtue of his being man, he is in the image of God; it is not dependent upon the presence of anything else. . . . Although very closely linked to the image of God, experiencing relationships and exercising dominion are not themselves that image.[24]

This universal substantive/essence view of the image of God seems to carry the most promise of providing the rationale for consistently upholding the sanctity of life in our contemporary situation. The fact that the image of God is a universal characteristic of all human beings leads to the truth that every person has inestimable value, inherent personal worth, and equality as a member of the human family. There is intrinsic dignity to being human. There is innate value in human life. And if this is so, then human life is sacred and deserves full consideration for protection and advocacy.

Spiritual Leaders Are Called to Advocacy

Finally, we need to examine a biblical basis for Christian ethical advocacy. Paul's letter to Philemon has been considered a theological anomaly by some scholars who have wondered why a private letter with little openly principle-oriented teaching should have been thought to have been inspired, especially when Paul does not claim apostolic authority for what he writes here. For instance, Joseph Fitzmyer writes, "Paul does not invoke his apostolic authority to demand obedience of Philemon."[25] With no apostolic authority claimed, perhaps the inclusion of the Letter to Philemon in the canon of scripture should have been dismissed. But when the Letter to Philemon is seen as an example of pastoral advocacy and as a model of expressing leadership concern in a difficult social/ethical dilemma, the letter comes alive in a new way and transcends the less important immediate context of what some have called a "religious response" to slavery. So let us set the scene and examine what faced Paul in this first-century ethical dilemma.

The apostle Paul probably wrote this letter from prison to a friend and convert in Colossae named Philemon, who was the owner of a runaway slave named Onesimus. Onesimus had met Paul in his travels and, in God's grace, had become a Christian under Paul's ministry (Philem. 10). Now Onesimus was willing to return to his master, make amends, and reconcile their relationship. Paul sent this letter with him to explain the new commitment Onesimus had made and to ask Philemon to receive him as a brother in the faith (v. 16). The structure of the letter is organized in the ancient Greek and Roman rhetorical style with a view toward persuading Philemon: (1) through recognition of prior relationship with Paul; (2) rational examination of facts; and (3) emotional appeal. The power of the letter comes from the insight it offers into Paul's compassion and understanding of leadership in the body of Christ as he advocates for a fellow believer in a difficult decision-making situation. Should the slave return? Or should he continue with Paul as a free man and with a new "ministry" as Christian coworker and helper? Would he be treated poorly upon return to his master, or even be put to death? The ethical dilemma of a slave/master relationship in Christ, complicated by loss of revenue (v. 19), presented itself to Paul, Onesimus, and eventually to Philemon. In Paul's letter of advocacy, there are two significant points that can be instructive for those seeking to be advocates in ethical contexts today.

First, the basis of Paul's advocacy for Onesimus was an *established pastoral relationship*. Paul had been the instrument of God in Onesimus's life by bringing him to Christ. Paul felt a personal commitment to his "son" (v. 10) in the faith. His personal love for Onesimus is detected when he writes, "I am sending him—who is my very heart—back to you" (v. 12). It is clear from the text that Paul had an established relationship with Onesimus. He loved Onesimus and wanted to protect him as a father would protect a son, or a guardian one under his care, or a pastor his flock. Similarly, Paul's relationship to Philemon was based upon a common life in Christ. Paul addresses his letter to "Philemon our dear friend and fellow worker" (v. 1). Later it is clear that Paul has known Philemon for an extended period of time and that he has heard reports of Philemon's work for the cause of Christ. He writes, "Your love has given me great joy and encouragement, because you, brother, have refreshed the hearts of the saints" (v. 7). A pastoral relationship is once again clearly evident, and Paul's advocacy is based upon that unique relationship.

Paul saw himself as an advocate for Christ and his kingdom and as a representative of the Christian "way." He many times encouraged Christians in the various locations and churches he visited to follow his model as they continued to mature in the faith. To the Corinthians he wrote, "Even though you have ten thousand guardians in Christ, you do not have many fathers, for in Christ Jesus I became your father through the gospel. Therefore I urge you to imitate me" (1 Cor. 4:15–16). When he lived with the Thessalonians, they too were encouraged to imitate his example: "For we know, brothers, loved by God, that he has chosen you, because our gospel came to you not simply with words, but also with power, with the Holy Spirit and with deep conviction. You know how we lived among you for your sake. You became imitators of us and of the Lord; in spite of severe suffering, you welcomed the message with the joy given by the Holy Spirit" (1 Thess. 1:6). And such is the admonition to Christians throughout scripture. The writer of the Letter to the Hebrews encouraged Christians: "Remember your leaders, who spoke the word of God to you. Consider the outcome of their way of life and imitate their faith" (Heb. 13:7). Paul was an advocate because he was a leader in Christ. Those who were in a *pastoral relationship* with him sought his counsel and welcomed his advice.

If you are a leader in your fellowship of believers, whether it be a church, a Bible study group, an informal group of Christian friends, or persons you know from your job, you can expect that they will seek your advice when confronted with life decisions that affect their Christian walk. If they are biblical Christians, they will seek out persons who are mature in the Lord in order to get their perspective on whatever crisis they are facing. When that happens you have an opportunity to be an influence for Jesus. 1 Peter 5:2 reminds "elders" that they are to "shepherd God's flock." If someone counts you as an "elder" in their life, then you can count it a blessing to be a possible instrument of God for them as you give witness to Jesus's way in your life. You become one they will look to imitate as you walk with them through their crisis.

Second, Paul's advocacy for Onesimus was characterized by *compassionate respect and acceptance.* This was demonstrated by his approach and by the way he related to Philemon and Onesimus. Instead of aggressively confronting Philemon with his own agenda of reinstating Onesimus, *not* as a slave but, conversely, as a brother in Christ, Paul "appealed" to Philemon with compassion to accept Onesimus. The open choice of what to do was left to Philemon, and to Philemon alone. J. J. Müller writes concerning Paul, "Although Paul has the right and the boldness in Christ, by merit of his apostolic authority, to command

Philemon to do what is befitting, and to prescribe what his plain duty was in this particular case, yet he rather requests, entreats, pleads with him as brother towards brother for love's sake."[26] Paul wrote, "Therefore, although in Christ I could be bold and order you to do what you ought to do, yet I appeal to you on the basis of love" (vv. 8–9). Here Paul models an advocacy approach that is noncoercive and respectful of others. Paul's approach is one of coming alongside to comfort and advise.[27] The word used by Paul in verse nine for "appeal" is the Greek word *parakalo*, which means to call to, to appeal, to exhort, to comfort.[28] James D. G. Dunn, in writing about Paul's use of this word, says that it "epitomizes the quality of discourse which should characterize the church in its discussion and debate—that is, not the demand of rights or threat of sanctions . . . but the exhortation, the appeal, the request within a community whose members trust and respect each other."[31]

Paul's is the best approach as an advocacy model for Christian leaders who want to be a comfort and a friend in tough medical ethics decision-making dilemmas. When we accompany someone to the ER or ICU, we cannot pretend to know all the aspects of the given situation or what is happening in the mind of our Christian decision maker. And we cannot just quote scripture and give pat answers when we are so completely in the dark about what might truly be occurring. We *can* certainly remember biblical truth and not compromise basics of what we know to be right and good and edifying in a Christian moral ethic. But we must be listening and hearing with wise ears the issues our friend finds to be significant and respect and accept his or her "light" on the things being faced. Most of all we must not be aggressive in promoting our agenda in the outcome. A noncoercive approach is the biblical approach for advocacy in difficult decision-making processes. I would encourage all those who seek to be an advocate to emulate the example Paul gives in his letter to Philemon. In times when decisions must be made, Christians have a tremendous resource at their disposal: the loving support of like-minded leaders who care. David E. Garland offers Christians good advice when he writes, "It may be helpful to have members of our church advise us in moral decisions that we now consider to be private matters. Left alone, we are more likely to make the wrong ethical decision. Surrounded by those who are committed to Christ and who pray together, we may be more likely to choose God's will. Our fellow Christians may be more toughminded in helping us put God's love to work in our lives."[30]

In summary, we have examined three important biblical themes related to medical ethics and Christian advocacy. We have located the foundation for ethics in the revealed character of God. For us, other sources of truth or mere human opinion fall short of providing a sure foundation upon which to stand. Second, the value of human life, with life's attendant dignity and respect, was shown to come *not* from a humanistic appeal to value, but from God's action in creation itself and the unique nature of human beings who carry the image of God in distinction to all other created life. Finally, a biblical model of advocacy for the Christian was examined in Paul's letter to Philemon. Christian leaders have a call to advocate for those under their ministry care. Next, we will examine the role of spirituality as it is viewed by medical practitioners and how diverse religious beliefs impact health-care decisions.

Notes

1. Peter Kreeft and Ronald K. Tacelli, *Handbook of Christian Apologetics* (Downers Grove, IL: InterVarsity Press, 1994), 364–65.

2. Ibid., 365.

3. Stanley J. Grenz, *The Moral Quest* (Downers Grove: InterVarsity Press, 1997), 241.

4. Christopher J. H. Wright, *An Eye for an Eye: The Place of Old Testament Ethics Today* (Downers Grove, IL: InterVarsity Press, 1983), 24.

5. Douglas R. Groothuis, *Truth Decay: Defending Christianity against the Challenges of Postmodernism* (Downers Grove, IL: InterVarsity Press, 2000), 193.

6. See Glenn McGee, ed., *Pragmatic Bioethics* (Nashville: Vanderbilt University Press, 1999).

7. For a history of the impact Dewey and Tufts have had upon American ethics discussion, see Daniel Callahan and Sissela Bok, eds., *Ethics Teaching in Higher Education* (New York: Plenum Press and The Hastings Center, 1980).

8. Stanley J. Grenz, *A Primer on Postmodernism* (Grand Rapids: Eerdmans, 1996), 163.

9. Ibid., 164.

10. Wright, *An Eye for an Eye,* 26–27.

11. A. D. Verhey, "New Testament Ethics," in *New Dictionary of Christian Ethics & Pastoral Theology,* ed. David J. Atkinson (Downers Grove, IL: InterVarsity Press, 1995), 57–58.

12. H. Tristram Engelhardt Jr., *The Foundations of Christian Bioethics* (Lisse, The Netherlands: Swets & Zeitlinger, 2000), 395.

13. See Millard J. Erickson, *Christian Theology* (Grand Rapids: Baker Books, 1984), 464.

14. Ibid., 464.

15. Grenz, *Moral Quest,* 258.

16. It is my practice to use *Man* with capitalization as representative of "man as male and female." The biblical use of *man* in Genesis 1:26–27 is as an inclusive word.

17. Walter Brueggemann, *Genesis*, Interpretation: A Biblical Commentary for Teaching and Preaching (Atlanta: John Knox, 1971), 31.

18. J. I. Packer, *Knowing God* (Downers Grove, IL: InterVarsity Press, 1973), 100.

19. For a discussion regarding Barth and Brunner's relational view of the "image of God," I recommend Erickson, *Christian Theology*, 502f.

20. Scott B. Rae and Paul M. Cox, *Bioethics: A Christian Approach in a Pluralistic Age* (Grand Rapids: Eerdmans, 1999), 131–32.

21. The word *essence* is used by Rae and Cox to capture the real and ultimate nature of Man's possession of the image of God, as opposed to the relational or capacity definitions of the image. See Rae and Cox, *Bioethics*, 132.

22. Francis Brown, S. R. Driver, and C. A. Briggs, *Hebrew and English Lexicon of the Old Testament*, 5th ed. (Oxford: Oxford University Press, 1977).

23. Rae and Cox, *Bioethics*, 133.

24. Erickson, *Christian Theology*, 513.

25. Joseph A. Fitzmyer, "The Letter to Philemon," in *The Jerome Biblical Commentary*, ed. Raymond E. Brown, Joseph A. Fitzmyer, and Roland E. Murphy (Englewood Cliffs, NJ: Prentice Hall, 1968), 333.

26. Jacobus Johannes Müller, *The Epistles of Paul to the Philippians and to Philemon* (Grand Rapids: Eerdmans, 1978), 179.

27. Cain Hope Felder, "The Letter to Philemon," in *The New Interpreter's Bible*, vol. 11 (Nashville: Abingdon Press, 2000), 898.

28. Gerhard Fredrich, ed. *Theological Dictionary of the New Testament*, vol. 5 (Grand Rapids: Eerdmans, 1967), 776.

29. James D. G. Dunn, *The Epistles to the Colossians and to Philemon*, The New International Greek Testament Commentary (Grand Rapids: Eerdmans, 1996), 326.

30. David E. Garland, *The NIV Application Commentary: Colossians/Philemon* (Grand Rapids: Zondervan, 1998), 323–24.

5

The Medical Understanding
of Spirituality

Jim was dying from lung cancer. He had worked hard all his life at a local industrial plant and had become financially successful over the years. Unfortunately, it had taken a toll physically, and he was left not only with cancer, but also with terrible arthritis and diabetes. When I made my first visit to his home he was in a wheelchair. The nurses warned me that Jim was a very angry man and that he had verbally struck out at them several times over the last weeks. They also said he was a Christian and that he was afraid to die. They expressed the hope that my visits would be able to help Jim with his anger and the anxiety he was experiencing in facing his death.

One of the most notable discoveries made during my time as a health-care chaplain has to do with how poorly many Christians are prepared to deal with the tragedies of life, such as the onset of a debilitating illness or the diagnosis of a terminal disease. It seems that their faith beliefs don't have enough depth to provide the strength they need in such times of crisis. Health-care professionals who regularly work with dying patients get a chance to see how a variety of the patients cope and adjust. There is a saying that goes: "People die just like they live." A man who lived as a tough "John Wayne type" in facing life's adversities would also face death or illness with courage and a stiff upper lip. Another person who through the years exhibited a life of "head-in-the-sand avoidance" wouldn't even want to know what might happen to him in the last weeks of his life. Some might opt for "gorking" medication and dream themselves into death, and others would simply never speak as if they would ever die. A person who lived a life of anger would die angry as a miserable human being, and a person who lived a life of laughter would die with laughter. Some people who were extroverts would want many people around them during the dying process, and others who were introverts would want few people to visit them in their last days. People do seem to die just as they have lived. But when a person is a Christian there is an expectation, often not mentioned but a reality nonetheless, that he or she will die with peace, quietness, and acceptance. Because we believe in the presence of Jesus and the reality of a heavenly home, everyone assumes that Christians will have a Spirit-born strength when facing death. This is not the case. I would always hear from the RNs (most of whom were probably not from a Christian background) about their "Christian" patients who were afraid to die, or who were angry and unaccepting of their illness, or who were in some way not acting with the faith they "should" have as a professed Christian. Most of the RNs saw this as a sign that Christianity was a self-serving religion with no real power or truth. After all, some non-Christian patients were facing death with more courage than those who professed to believe! I could only agree that somehow the real essence of their faith had not been internalized in these patients. When the proverbial rubber hit the road, faith was absent. I certainly was aware of the poor witness that was being left as these patients interacted with their caregivers. The patients themselves probably never thought a thing about the impression their actions were leaving.

My conversations with Jim were very friendly and mutually enjoyable. I could tell he liked me, and I genuinely liked him. That first visit he related the story of his life and the importance of his Christian commitment. He became a Christian through the influence of his wife, Lois. He raised three children in the church and expressed his personal joy in the fact that they had all married Christian spouses and were still active in church and were raising their own children "in the faith." Jim had some carpentry skills and took pride in the fact that he helped work on the new church worship center. He had been a trustee throughout that period and a church leader. He related that he didn't attend many Bible studies or extra events because he was not a "group" person. As a good chaplain I listened to his story and offered prayer at the end of the visit, emphasizing our belief in the presence of Jesus and the strength we have through God's power and not our own. Jim asked me to come back, and so a new pastoral relationship was born.

When I visited him again I was able to ask him more about how he was facing his coming death. He was very open about how betrayed he felt at the suddenness of the physical decline. He told me that he was angry and that he had "taken it out on" the nurses. He hoped they would understand that he was not himself and that he was under a lot of stress. His body was going downhill very quickly. Within the last two weeks he had lost his ability to walk and was forced into the wheelchair. He knew that soon he would be bedridden and unable to do some of the activities that he enjoyed even now. He was a gardener, and beautiful flower beds surrounded their home. The opportunity to be outdoors, to work the dirt, and to admire God's creation in the beautiful flowers had provided a sense of God's care and presence for him over the last weeks. He wondered what would happen to the flowers when he could no longer tend to them. He would also miss just being out amid God's creation. It was an anticipated loss that was weighing heavily upon him.

When I asked Jim if he prayed much, he confessed, "I used to pray all the time, but lately God has seemed so distant. That's why I liked the prayer we shared on your last visit. It gave me strength." Upon further questioning, as I sought to get a picture of his personal spiritual resources, he stated that he felt very assured that there was an after-life. He believed in heaven and knew he would go immediately to "be with Jesus" when he died. He also said that he believed in angels, and that he had met one! I was intrigued by this information and so asked him to explain. He related that an angel had visited him one evening just a week ago after he went to bed. He said that he was lying quietly when the room became "lighted up" and a figure was positioned at the foot of his bed. He couldn't see the face, but he remembered the words that were spoken: "You are under my protection. Do not fear." The figure reached out and touched his ankles. Jim told me that an undeniable feeling of peace and well-being flooded him and that espe-cially his legs became very warm! He went on to explain that his legs had been chronically cold over the last weeks because of increasingly poor circulation. Now they were warm. Significantly, this "appearance" was something more than an hallucination. It had a physical "sign" associated with it. The visit was something that gave Jim strength over the last weeks of his life.

Jim died about three weeks later. I was called by Lois when the nurse thought Jim's time was close. We prayed and sat with him for a short while as he struggled to breathe. Suddenly his eyes opened; he looked straight up toward the ceiling and said, "It's beautiful." Those were his last words. He was gone.

Jim's anger had subsided after the visit by the angel, and a growing acceptance that he would be "OK" had been evident in his speech and demeanor. His nurses noticed the difference in his outward personality and even brought it to my attention. They wondered what had made him change. His family experienced Jim's death and testimony about the angel as a strong witness of the reality of God and of spiritual things. It was ironic that this Christian man was perceived at first as being so "un-Christian" by his attending caregivers.

Spirituality and Spiritual Resources

Jim's story illustrates the truth that being a Christian in and of itself does not necessarily prepare us for life's challenges. It is our personal "spirituality" that provides the resources we need when crises occur. I would like to suggest a practical understanding of *spirituality* as the "tool kit" of faith resources and practices we develop in our lives, and to which we turn when we need God's presence and strength. Jim's spirituality was not able at first to meet the challenges of a terminal diagnosis. He was not prepared to deal with the fact that his life would be much shorter than he had hoped. He became angry at God and angry at his caregivers, which probably resulted in some depression and, certainly, a very observable anxiety. These may be natural human responses to a terrible new reality, but the fact that Jim was unprepared spiritually is still significant. After several months he was able to build a spirituality that helped him cope. Or maybe he was just made aware of aspects of his Christian walk that he hadn't really internalized previously. His spirituality came to be characterized by a belief in heaven, a belief in prayer, a belief in angels, and a trust in God's love for him through Jesus. He also relied upon love of family and the spiritual strength he received while gardening and reflecting upon the beauty of God's creation. The visit by the angel served to solidify his trust in a God who is *really there* and who could be trusted to protect him even through the experience of death. God's supernatural power as experienced in the warming of his legs was an important resource Jim could draw upon as he anticipated death.

Pastors and Christian leaders need to know that spirituality is a significant factor in medical ethics and in medical decision making. However, it is a word that is used in many contexts in our contemporary society, by many different people, and with many different meanings attached. Eugene Peterson writes of the word *spirituality* that it "sounds the note of comprehensiveness—anything and everything that men and women designate as they speak or think about the significance of their lives, including God and personal meaning and concern for the world."[1] Although spirituality has a biblical and historical meaning for the Christian, it *is* important for us to be aware of the specifically medical understanding of spirituality and its significance for health-care professionals in today's medical setting. Christian leaders can be well grounded in foundational moral principles, have a strong personal commitment to the sanctity of life and inherent human dignity, and feel the call to advocacy, and yet be unfamiliar with medical perspectives of spirituality and its influence upon patients in the health-care setting. Therefore, we will now define spirituality as it is typically understood in the medical setting, examine how personal spirituality can make a difference in patient care, and review the institutional mandate to provide spiritual care in today's medical centers—all with a view toward educating ourselves to be better Christian advocates for those who rely upon us as their spiritual support persons.

Medical professionals define spirituality in cognitive, experiential, and behavioral terms. Especially helpful is the description suggested by Gowri Anandarajah and Ellen Hight:

> Spirituality is a complex and multidimensional part of the human experience. It has cognitive, experiential and behavioral aspects. The cognitive or philosophic aspects include search for meaning, purpose and truth in life and the beliefs and values by which an individual lives. The experiential and emotional aspects involve feelings of hope, love, connection, inner peace, comfort and support. These are reflected in the quality of an individual's inner resources, and the ability to give and receive spiritual love, and the types of relationships and connections that exist with self, the community, the environment and nature, and the transcendent (e.g., power greater than self, a value system, God, cosmic consciousness). The behavioral aspects of spirituality involve the way a person externally manifests individual spiritual beliefs and inner spiritual state. Many persons find spirituality through religion or through a personal relationship with the divine. However, others may find it through a connection to nature, through music and the arts, through a set of values and principles or through a quest for scientific truth.[2]

In a health-care setting, we can think of spirituality as being concerned with *how* a person uses (or practices) his or her religion. In contrast, "religion" is often viewed among medical professionals as a separate entity that *includes* personal spirituality, but with the addition of a moral code, creeds, rituals, organized worship patterns, and a community of faith or congregation. A religion can usually be identified by name, for example, Christian, Jewish, Hindu, Islamic, etc., whereas spirituality concerns *practices* that are person-specific and individualistic in nature.

A second helpful understanding of spirituality is suggested by the North American Nursing Diagnosis Association (NANDA) in their recognition of the role of spirituality in the healing process and of the incidence of what is called "spiritual distress." Spiritual distress is a diagnostic category in nursing and is defined as "disruption in the life principle that pervades a person's entire being and that integrates and transcends one's biological and psychosocial nature."[3] In regard to the diagnosis of "spiritual distress" (or the crisis one may enter when spiritual beliefs are challenged by medical realities) NANDA lists as defining characteristics the following:

> Expresses concern with meaning of life/death and/or belief systems (critical); questions moral/ethical implications of therapeutic regimen; description of nightmares/sleep disturbances; verbalizes inner conflict about beliefs; verbalizes concern about relationship with deity; unable to participate in usual religious practices; seeks spiritual assistance; questions meaning of suffering; questions meaning of own existence; displacement of anger toward religious representatives; anger toward God; alteration in behavior/mood evidenced by anger, crying, withdrawal, preoccupation, anxiety, hostility, apathy, etc.: gallows humor.[4]

In this definition, spiritual distress (or spirituality) has to do with such things as personal significance, life purpose, meaning derived from existence, relationship with transcendence, and personal faith that integrates one's life activities. So, to illustrate, everyone has a need to know that their life has personal significance and makes a difference in the world. And everyone has a need to know that someone cares about them, that they are loved, and that they serve a purpose in life. And they have a need to know that God accepts them in their doubting, and anger, and questioning, and anxiety, and fearfulness. This definition assumes that it is an integrative human spiritual concern that answers the questions "What is the meaning of life?" and "Why is this suffering happening to me?" Once again the emphasis in the NANDA definition is upon a patient's *personal* spirituality and personal understanding of these questions as opposed to adherence to any organized religion. But for us, the existence of this diagnostic category points to the importance that personal spirituality holds in contemporary health care. The reason spiritual distress is addressed in diagnostic literature is that spirituality has been found to be a significant contributor to overall healing and health.

Spirituality and Health

Research in the area of spirituality and healing is on the cutting edge when it comes to recent interests of health-care professionals. Much has been written in the last few years about the importance of prayer in the healing process. Continuing studies have attempted to document the importance of personal spirituality to health. A distinguished group of Mayo Clinic researchers, in speaking of the importance of spirituality to medicine today, has noted:

> In Western medicine, after the 1600s, science claimed the "body" and relegated the "soul" to spiritual or religious beliefs and practices. Today, we continue to see evidence of this classification as the science of medicine and spiritual beliefs are often considered to be disparate or mutually exclusive. However, medical science alone fails to address a vital element of human experience as up to 98 percent of hospitalized patients describe a belief in God or some higher power, and 96 percent acknowledge a personal use of prayer to aide in the healing process.[5]

To this insight, thoughtful Christians can only say "Yes!" and wonder why it has taken so long. But more and more physicians from Christian and other faith backgrounds are observing patients and noting the importance that spirituality has in their hospital experience. And, more important, they are not as quick to disregard spirituality or minimize its role simply because it is something different from biological or physical science. Instead, spirituality is beginning to be seen as an essential piece of human experience in the healing process.

A 2001 comprehensive study of medical research in the area of spirituality by another group of Mayo Clinic physicians reviewed published studies, research analyses, and other clinical papers associated with spiritual influence upon health-related quality of life (HRQOL). They report: "A majority of the nearly 350 studies of physical health and 850 studies of mental health that have used religious and spiritual variables have found that religious involvement and spirituality are associated with better health outcomes."[6] Many of the studies have indicated a "direct relationship" between spirituality and better health outcomes even after accounting for other personal health habits.[7] Paul Mueller and colleagues' study included a large sampling of U.S. adults (up to 22,080 adults) and was adjusted for such variables as age, sex, marital status, ethnicity, education, baseline health status, body mass index, health practices (exercise, smoking), social connections, income levels, employment status, and more. In each study the incidence of death was significantly *lower* for frequent church attenders during the follow-up period than for non-attenders.[8] In addition to mortality studies, a variety of recent research has demonstrated that spirituality and spiritual practices lead to more positive heath outcomes with cardiovascular disease, hypertension, depression, anxiety, substance abuse, and suicide.[9] "Like other factors that promote health (e.g., exercise), religious involvement and spirituality likely enhance resistance to disease through the interaction of multiple beneficial mediators."[10] No wonder physicians are beginning to look at the personal spiritual commitments of the patients they treat!

An ensuing finding that impacts medical decision making specifically has to do with the enhanced coping abilities in illness or during stress as a result of personal spirituality. Positive emotions resulting from religious/spiritual participation such as "hope, love, contentment, and forgiveness, have psychological effects (e.g., less anxiety) and physiological effects (e.g., decreased blood pressure, heart rate, and oxygen consumption)"[11] and may, it seems, lead to greater optimism, less hostility, and better acceptance of the family/patient/physician relationship. In other words, spirituality may contribute to the comfort experienced by the patient and to the comfort level experienced by family decision makers as they address the care of the patient. They are able to cope better. A patient's spirituality "enhances coping . . . during illness; it can be a source of identity, meaning, purpose, hope, reassurance, and transcendence, and it can mitigate the uncertainties of illness."[12] In citing these findings, it is clear that spirituality has an effect upon positive patient outcomes, upon healing, and upon wholeness. Spirituality also brings a greater comfort level to decision makers as they struggle with varieties of treatment options to help the patient. But personal spirituality can also bring complications to the human experience of illness or healing. At times a patient's personal beliefs and spiritual commitments can indirectly cause additional personal suffering or other seemingly incongruent outcomes, as illustrated in the following example of spirituality in practice.

Personal Spirituality in Practice

John was a Bible-believing Baptist who was very serious about his faith and call to serve God. He entered our medical center's comfort care wing after several months of attempting to ward off an aggressive bone cancer centered in his pelvis and legs. When I made an initial visit to meet John on my way through that part of the hospital, we immediately built a good relationship and I visited him many times over the next weeks. On one of those visits I heard from John's RN that he had refused pain medication and that he was really suffering that day. She wanted me to go and talk with him and, hopefully, get him to accept medication to ease his pain. When I entered his room John was sitting up in bed, hugging his pillow, and bending back and forth while reciting scripture from memory. Around his eyes pain had etched small lines. He was definitely hurting. When I inquired about his refusal of the pain medication, he said, "I want to experience all that Jesus wants me to experience, even if it is suffering. He died for me on the cross, and I want to live for him with every breath I take." John went on to explain that he felt called to suffer with Christ so that he would be "refined as by fire" and made pure in faith as he prepared to meet his Lord in heaven. He named several Bible verses that were important to him. They included:

> Dear friends, do not be surprised at the painful trial you are suffering, as though something strange were happening to you. But rejoice that you participate in the sufferings of Christ, so that you may be overjoyed when his glory is revealed.
>
> 1 Peter 4:12–13

> In this you greatly rejoice, though now for a little while you may have had to suffer grief in all kinds of trials. These have come so that your faith—of greater worth than gold, which perishes even though refined by fire—may be proved genuine and may result in praise, glory and honor when Jesus Christ is revealed.
>
> 1 Peter 1:6–7

Now if we are children, then we are heirs—heirs of God and co-heirs with Christ, if indeed we share in his sufferings in order that we may also share in his glory.

Romans 8:17

For just as the sufferings of Christ flow over into our lives, so also through Christ our comfort overflows.

2 Corinthians 1:5

John knew that God would give him strength to fight off the pain. He was very serious about his commitment to suffer. This was an important part of his Christian faith and personal spirituality. We held hands and I prayed with him that day as he sought the courage to do what he believed God expected of him as a faithful believer. I went out to the RN and told her that he would probably never accept a higher dose of medication. She was absolutely shocked at his decision to bear the pain *and* that it was a *religious* belief behind this idea! She spoke to the doctor. Several patient-care conferences ensued in which John (with me at his side) had to insist on his right to pain, and which were all eventually resolved in John's favor. It was an ethical leap for the RN and the physician to accept that their patient did not want pain relief. To them it felt like they were "doing harm" and not fulfilling their ethical commitment to alleviate pain in the tradition of the beneficence and nonmaleficence principles. I explained to them the theological and personal rationale behind his decision. In this example, a patient's personal spirituality was in conflict with the commitments of the care team and actually resulted in more suffering and pain for the patient. But it was the patient's desires that were determinative and of primary significance. John died having accepted no pain control and with the joy of the Lord on his lips.

Though our hospital served a generally homogeneous population, spiritual issues would always arise as patients and their families brought individual spiritual commitments with them when they were admitted for treatment. A large Native American population in the area added an interesting twist when "Christian" Native Americans would combine their Christian beliefs with a variety of traditional spiritualities and family values. Sometimes they would request a special picture of an animal "spirit guide" to be placed near their bed in the intensive care unit, or beautiful personal blankets from home would be brought into the sterile environment of the hospital room to help the Native American patient feel surrounded by healing power. The blanket and the spirit guide would be accompanied by pictures of Jesus and a cross or crucifix. These practices might seem a little unusual for the normal Christian pastor or priest, but they are common issues for those who minister within the variety of cultures present in different regions of our diverse society. Music was often requested, and the hospital had several CD players available for patients and families to use as they attempted to provide a patient in critical condition with an appropriate and spiritually sensitive healing environment. Pastors and other Christian advocates can be assured that the hospital staff are willing to do whatever they can to provide the spiritual resources requested by a patient. This is part of the medical staff's commitment to meet the patient's and family's spiritual needs. Hospital chaplains can be a resource for families with special needs, as well as an important supportive resource for visiting pastors or elders.

Sometimes we are requested by our church families or friends to make hospital calls (or advocate) for patients with no church or congregational membership. My experience with Nancy is an example of just such a patient. I have found that when I honor the spiritual practices of someone with whom I have no personal relationship (without compromising my own Christian commitments) that conversations about spirituality can lead to additional personal openness and the opportunity for both persons to learn from each other. Nancy had come to our Same Day Surgery center to have some soft tissue removed. She was Caucasian but followed the spiritual practice of sweetgrass burning. Sweetgrass is a native grass that is cut and bundled for ceremonial purposes. I was called by the surgery staff because she was insisting on burning sweetgrass as a spiritual practice before her procedure, and the staff was resistant. Ten or twelve other patients were located in the same waiting area, with only a curtain separating them. The staff felt that the smoke from burning the sweetgrass would infringe on the other patients' privacy and their rights to clean air. Plus, they could see that this particular patient was not Native American and so were suspicious of her request. Regardless, Nancy had the right to practice her faith before her surgery. I saw my involvement as an opportunity not only to advocate for Nancy and perhaps build a bridge of friendship, but also to educate the surgery staff on the importance of patients' rights and sensitivity to spiritual values.

So I introduced myself to Nancy and asked her about her spiritual commitments. She told me about the importance of daily prayer and daily purification in her life, and the role that the sweetgrass burning had in her personal spirituality. Every morning she would start the day by giving thanks to the Creator and by burning sweetgrass in prayer. The request to do it in the hospital was only in keeping with her normal routine, except that she *was* a little frightened about the surgery procedure and wanted to be spiritually centered before undergoing it. She knew she would feel a comfort and strength from recognizing the power of the Creator in her life before having the surgery.

I went to the RN staff and advocated for this patient's right to practice her spirituality. The manager of the department suggested that one way to satisfy Nancy and to protect other patients was to move Nancy into the one private "ready room" available in the Same Day Surgery area. It had a door that could be closed. If we could make this move, I was confident that the amount of smoke would be minimal and that the impact on other patients would be nil. So Nancy was moved to the ready room and given permission to do her ritual. Since I had not ever seen a person burn sweetgrass, I asked Nancy if I could join her as she did it. She wholeheartedly invited me to be present.

She sat up in the bed, took out a pouch that had a short tuft of sweetgrass about two inches in diameter and four inches long, a box of matches, and a small metal plate on which to set the burning grass. She struck the match, held it to the sweetgrass for ten seconds, and blew on it to make the tuft smolder. Then, in a sequence of movements that lasted about twenty seconds, she rotated the smoking grass around the top of her head, under her hair around her neck, around her torso, and around and under both arms. She then moved it down the length of both legs, back up and around her head again, and finally reached for the plate and extinguished the burning grass by smashing the tuft on the plate. All of this was done silently and reverently. At that point she looked at me and thanked me for allowing her to complete her prayer and purification. I thanked her for allowing me to watch. She then said, "Now I feel better about having my surgery." I felt good that she was able to do this thing that was obviously so important to her.

When I left Nancy and went to tell the staff that the ritual was completed, Nancy's RN was upset and said, "The smoke came out of the room and was so strong that one of my staff had to move to the other side of the ward because of her sensitivity and tendency for asthma." The implication was that other patients were probably also affected by the smoke. The RN said to me, "This will never happen in our unit again." I was disappointed in her response, and I had a hard time believing that the smoke was *that* intrusive. Even in the separate room during the burning I was not at all bothered by the small amount of smoke generated. I wondered if the one RN was just acting upset in order to make a point. Later that day I spoke to our hospital risk manager about the incident and he upheld the importance of the patient's right to this ritual. To my knowledge no patient in the unit complained about smoke affecting their breathing that day. This was no doubt the first time such a request had been honored in our Same Day Surgery department. Nancy's request provided a good learning experience for the staff and is an example of some of the opposition that an advocate might experience in the hospital setting. Once again, the hospital chaplain in any conflicted situation is a good resource and support for the visiting pastor.

Patients' Rights, the Ethics Committee, and Spiritual Advocacy

Nancy's request is a good example of the type of spiritual expression that medical centers are mandated to honor as part of their accreditation by the Joint Commission on Accreditation of Healthcare Organizations (JCAHO). This organization is the national accreditation group for hospitals and other health-care organizations. It accredits many hospitals but not all. Still, even nonaccredited hospitals use many of the JCAHO standards as general rules of practice. It is important for spiritual leaders to know a little about where the protection of the spiritual values of patients can be found. Under the Patients' Rights and Organizational Ethics guidelines, JCAHO requires compliance with the following standard: "Patients have a fundamental right to considerate care that safeguards their personal dignity and respects their cultural, psychological, and spiritual values."[13] The respecting of spiritual values centers on meeting patients' needs for rituals, spiritual resources, and spiritual support from their spiritual leaders.

JCAHO is also very clear in requiring accredited hospitals to invite and welcome the involvement of spiritual-care professionals and the personal clergy (or spiritual leaders/advocates) of patients when decision making is needed. Three specific areas are particularly singled out for spiritual-leader referral: (1) resolving ethical issues, (2) end-of-life care, and (3) organ donation concerns. In these situations a referral to a spiritual caregiver is on the top of the protocol list. As an example of the implementation of this standard, JCAHO swings wide the door for spiritual advocacy involvement by stating: "Hospital policy directs clinicians to refer family members to appropriate clergy or other organizational spiritual advisor for consultation when the issue of withholding resuscitative services arises."[14] In my work in the hospital it has been a common practice to invite a patient's minister to physician/family conferences and to other decision-making meetings when patients desire the support of their pastor or elder to make a hard decision. The JCAHO standards are meant to ensure that medical centers across the country welcome religious leaders as an important support for patients and families who face ethical dilemmas and health-care decisions. The standards also help ensure that patients and families who come to the hospital with diverse values and religious commitments receive care congruent with their personal beliefs.

If, as in Nancy's situation, there are hospital or staff concerns that other patients might be negatively affected by a spiritual practice, or issues that present conflicts of interests, or ethical dilemmas involving patient care and conflict of values, another resource for the spiritual leader is the hospital ethics committee. Ethics committees are found in many hospitals, but again not all. Ethics committees are instituted to be readily available for consultation by physicians, staff, patients, and families, for the safeguarding of patients' and families' rights, as well as the rights of the hospital. By JCAHO standards, all patients and families who are admitted to the medical center are to be *informed* of the existence of the ethics committee as well as *how* it can be accessed and a consultation requested. Hospital chaplains and social workers are good sources of referral for the ethics committee and can be found in any hospital by simply dialing the hospital operator.

The medical ethics committee is composed of a variety of caregivers from multiple disciplines involved in patient care. Members might be physicians, nurses, respiratory therapists, dietitians, attorneys, administrators, social workers, and chaplains/clergy. Such an interdisciplinary team is able to bring to consultations perspectives from a variety of viewpoints, to set the context for a reduced technical approach, and to ensure an objective critique of the views of any particular group or perspective. Usually members of the ethics committee are among the most sensitive and compassionate persons in the medical center. They are good listeners, respectful and accepting of a variety of viewpoints, and aware of relevant issues related to patient care and institution policies. Ethics committees follow an open, nonthreatening, and inclusive approach that values diversity and seeks to help patients and families have a positive hospital experience. I would encourage spiritual leaders to utilize the ethics committee whenever perceived conflicts in patient care present themselves.

What we have seen, then, is that the medical community defines spirituality in a practical and person-specific way that emphasizes *how* someone practices his or her personal beliefs or religious commitments. This personal spirituality is recognized by health-care professionals as an important piece of patient care, and the right of each patient to practice personal spirituality is protected in patients' rights documents and by JCAHO standards. These rights are generally accepted in medical centers everywhere. Patients' and families' values, faith commitments, and traditions are recognized as significant contributors to patient health and wholeness.

In addition, an understanding of the medical definition of personal spirituality is among the educational prerequisites for ministers equipping themselves for patient advocacy. Each minister should think about his or her own personal spirituality and be able to explain why it is important in their own relationship with God. Spirituality joins with our operational value system, our traumatic memory history, and our theological and biblical commitments to yield a fourfold integrated "personal advocacy profile" of which we need to be aware as we enter into helping others with the ethical dilemmas they are facing. There are always new twists and unusual circumstances, with particularly intriguing variables, that present themselves in patient-care situations. But ministers, elders, and other religious leaders can anticipate several frequently encountered situations with potential ethical problems for patients and families. It is to these that we now turn.

Notes

1. Eugene H. Peterson, *Christ Plays in Ten Thousand Places* (Grand Rapids: Eerdmans, 2005), 26.

2. Gowri Anandarajah and Ellen Hight, "Spirituality and Medical Practice: Using the HOPE Questions as a Practical Tool for Spiritual Assessment," *American Family Physician* 63, no. 1 (January 2001): 83.

3. North American Nursing Diagnosis Association, *Nursing Diagnoses: Definitions & Classification, 1999–2000* (Philadelphia: NANDA, 1999), 67.

4. Ibid., 67.

5. Jennifer M. Aviles, Sr. Ellen Whelan, Debra A. Hernke, Brent A. Williams, Kathleen E. Kenny, W. Michael O'Fallon, and Stephen L. Kopecky, "Intercessory Prayer and Cardiovascular Disease Progression in a Coronary Care Unit Population: A Randomized Controlled Trial," *Mayo Clinic Proceedings* 76 (2001): 1192.

6. Paul S. Mueller, David J. Plevak, and Teresa A. Rummans, "Religious Involvement, Spirituality, and Medicine: Implications for Clinical Practice," *Mayo Clinic Proceedings* 76 (2001): 1226.

7. H. G. Koenig, E. Idler, S. Kasl, et. al., "Religion, Spirituality, and Medicine: A Rebuttal to Skeptics," *International Journal of Psychology and Medicine* 29 (1999): 123–31.

8. Mueller, "Religious Involvement, Spirituality, and Medicine," 1226–27.

9. Ibid., 1227–28.

10. Ibid., 1229.

11. Ibid.

12. Ibid., 1231.

13. Patient's Rights and Organizational Ethics RI.1 *Overview, Comprehensive Accreditation Manual for Hospitals* (Chicago: JCAHO, 2000).

14. Patient's Rights and Organizational Ethics, RI.1.2.3. Subsequent JCAHO standards have moved away from this wording in the Elements of Performance but continue to emphasize the importance of meeting the patient's and family's need for appropriate spiritual care and support. See RI 2.10 and PC 8.7 of the *Hospital Accreditation Standards 2006* (Oakbrook Terrace, IL: JCAHO Publications, 2006).

6

Frequently Encountered
Ethical Problems

The ethical problems most often faced by patients and families in local hospitals usually do not have to do with global human issues—genetic testing, experimental procedures, fetal research, or human cloning. Though Christians everywhere should seek to be informed about the latest challenges of medical technology and come to some thoughtful conclusions for themselves based on God's revelation and personal convictions, these issues are not the ones that will be most important as we meet our friends and families in caregiving situations at our community medical centers. Instead, we will usually be facing ethical dilemmas surrounding things such as end-of-life choices, alternatives in patient treatment, withdrawal or withholding of life-support measures, organ donation, truth telling, informed consent, and patients' rights. To begin our look at ethical dilemmas, the significant learning point for the aspiring Christian advocate is the *recognition* of an ethical dilemma when it surfaces in a caregiving context. Just the mere recognition of an ethical dilemma is the first hurdle.

This is not just a problem faced by pastors. Medical professionals struggle with recognizing ethical problems and with putting words to their feelings that something "wrong" has occurred. Ethics researchers Ann Cook, Helena Hoas, and Jane Clare Joyner relate this example given by a nurse in a rural hospital:

> One nurse recalled a particularly difficult episode when she helped administer a very painful procedure to a man who was near death. In spite of the patient's strong objections, the doctor proceeded to administer the treatment. As the nurse explained, "I came back the next day. I was so upset, I hadn't slept. The staff were calling each other. I met with the director of nurses and told her what happened. But nothing ever happened. The issue never got addressed. There was no resolution for any of us involved in that night." For that nurse the episode was a turning point because it helped her recognize the ethical implications of the problem she faced.[1]

This nurse had strong personal feelings about the treatment given her dying patient. The physician was probably not wrong in any professional sense, but the unnecessary pain the patient suffered obviously bothered the nurse immensely. Cook and Hoas, in seeking to help caregivers identify their feelings, have developed a "moral distress scale" to assist those involved in patient treatment decisions in analyzing their ethical tension in situations. The moral distress scale is just a ten-point scale ranging from "no distress" to "worst possible, unbearable distress." It is based on the premise that we need to learn to listen to gut feelings as we are involved with patients about *what* happens to them or what *may* happen to them.

Religious leaders must also learn to listen to their gut feelings when involved in a patient's decision-making situation. If something strikes you as incongruent or distressing or wrong, then those feelings need to be identified and the issues verbalized as much as possible to aid in clarifying the source of the personal moral distress. Then, if you can put some *principles* out on the table that you think apply (doing good, sanctity of life, informed consent), or personal values important to the situation from your *operational value system,* you are well on the way to self-understanding and to being an informed and sensitive advocate.

A very difficult situation happened one day in the ER. A fifty-year-old man stabbed himself in the abdomen because of the constant pain he was experiencing related to terminal bone cancer. The pain had been unrelieved by any medical therapy. Paramedics brought him to the ER after a friend, who happened to be in the home when the patient stabbed himself, called them. Although the patient needed immediate aggressive medical care to keep from dying right then, neither the patient (who was still alert and oriented) nor his wife, who arrived shortly after the patient, wanted him to be given any treatment other than pain control. A quick review of his hospital chart confirmed that his oncology physicians were at a loss as to how to alleviate his pain and that he was expected to die within the next several weeks.

Ultimately, this patient was given enough pain medicine in the ER, at the request of his wife, to put him to sleep. She was assured he was in no pain. He died as expected an hour later from blood loss. A pastor who was an acquaintance of the patient was called by the wife to be at the hospital and was present for the death. After the patient died he was very upset that the patient had not been treated and hospitalized. At the time, he was uncertain why he felt upset. How would you have felt if you had been present? What aspects of this situation would bother you? Legally, the wife of the patient was the decision maker once the patient was unable to express his own desires. The ER doctor looked to her to provide guidance for her husband's care. She probably felt very compassionate toward her husband after witnessing the days of suffering he had endured and the inability of the doctors to control his pain. To actually make the decision to let him go was, no doubt, very hard for her, yet she related that she did it because she loved her husband and couldn't bear to see him go on like that given his cancer, the new wound, and the pain he would suffer. She knew that he also wanted to be relieved of his pain. When he died she was at peace, assured that his wishes had been followed. Later the pastor was able to share his thoughts on why he was upset with the way the death went. He saw the patient acting with suicidal intent. The patient's suicidal intent was a primary rationale in his feelings that the patient should have received treatment. His theological understanding told him that the patient's eternal destiny could be affected by a suicidal death. For that reason alone he wanted the man to live beyond this stabbing. To live in pain and die within the next several weeks was deemed more desirable by this pastor, whose spiritual beliefs provided the foundational point of reference in his decision. On the other hand, the ER staff, in talking among themselves, thought that the patient should never have come to the ER in the first place! If the well-meaning friend had just let him die at home, the dilemma of deciding whether treatment was "doing good" or "doing harm" could just be avoided. They all expressed sadness that his pain could not be controlled. Death was certain in his case. The only question was *by what means* and *how soon*. Such are the dilemmas of modern medical practice.

Deontological and Consequentialist Perspectives

In dealing with such ethical dilemmas there are two ethical perspectives proposed by Stanley Grenz that have helped me to understand how people view ethical dilemmas and think about possible solutions. These two ethical perspectives, the deontological approach and the consequentialist approach, are in continual tension with each other. The deontological perspective finds its starting point in considering whether an act is intrinsically right or wrong. The Greek word *deon*, or "what is due," focuses on one's absolute duty to do what is right based on universal rule or standard. For instance, "divine command" adherents believe absolute standards have been revealed by God and that an instituted moral law exists by which an action is "right" and people are "good" if and only if they obey the law.[2] In a different approach to the same deontological perspective, Immanuel Kant (1724–1804) suggested an ethical principle called the "categorical imperative," which asserts that an act is immoral if the law that would authorize it cannot be made into a rule for all human beings to follow. Kant believed that human beings have a unique ability to act in accordance with rules, laws, and principles regardless of interests or consequences.[3] Deontological proponents agree that consequences do not and should not enter into deciding whether actions are moral or immoral.

Consequentialist reasoning, on the other hand, focuses on the consequences of the act, according to Grenz. According to this perspective, decisions are to be made with the ultimate goal or consequences of an action in mind. Hopefully, the end result brings positive consequences to those involved, or at least the intent is to maximize the good and to reach the most desirable final consequence. Grenz summarizes this approach when he writes, "Our duty is to do that act which will bring about the greatest amount of good and the least amount of evil—that act which will result in the greatest balance of good over evil."[4]

This, no doubt simplified but helpful, ethical dichotomy is useful whenever ethical dilemmas are being debated and opposing sides are having trouble communicating. It is very helpful for a third party to attempt to locate the opposing adherents' viewpoints within one or the other of these foundational perspectives. Often persons on opposite sides of the ethical debate will be using one or the other of these two foundational perspectives and will be talking past each other without understanding the communication problem. Each group's arguments appear so bizarre to the other side that they question the other's rational thinking ability! In contrast, their own arguments seem self-evident. However, it is just the difference in the deontological and consequentialist perspectives that polarizes their arguments and inhibits communication.

An example of this type of dichotomous thinking is illustrated in the following abortion dilemma.[5] Imagine a young mother being informed after an ultrasound that she has an anencephalic baby in utero. Anencephaly is the absence of the brain other than the brain stem. Most often the entire top of the baby's head is missing. It is a condition "incompatible with life." An advisor following the deontological perspective, and with strong feelings that abortion is against universal moral law, would encourage the mother to keep the baby to term because "abortion does not uphold sanctity of life, and all life is precious." A second advisor, following the consequentialist perspective, would suggest that the baby be aborted: "Your baby will have to suffer, the baby will not live anyway, and you will be put through trauma and financial burdens you need not experience." I know of a situation similar to this in which the mother was a Christian and expressed her feelings that she did not want her baby to suffer. She did not believe that God would want the baby to be born just to suffer and die. This mother elected to have her baby aborted. People could empathize with either the deontological or the consequentialist position in this situation. It is particularly ironic that the mother felt her Christian duty was to minimize the suffering of her baby, even if it meant an abortion. If you found yourself having to make that decision, or found yourself in a situation where you were providing pastoral support to someone you care about, an important communication tool and educational learning piece would be to determine for all stakeholders which ethical perspective is being raised by conflicting advisors, whether deontological or consequentialist, and help them break through that significant communication barrier.

The importance of understanding these two perspectives is grounded in the fact that two equally well-meaning and committed Christians may indeed hold opposing viewpoints and do so within the framework of a truly biblical theology. In many ethical dilemmas there are various shades of gray manifested instead of true blacks and true whites. Christians on opposite sides of an argument need to be able to appreciate each other's perspectives, to dialogue, to seek understanding, and even if there is no agreement, at least to treat the other's stance and choice with respect and honor. More important, if a pastor/advocate were to disagree with a fellow Christian coming at the dilemma from the opposite perspective, and verbalized the disagreement, there might be the potential for "negative advocacy," where the parishioner might feel judged instead of supported, or even a break in the pastoral relationship. In such delicate circumstances it is much better to be humble in our approach and follow the apostle Paul's example in Philemon of compassionate respect and honoring of the other, rather than claiming "apostolic authority" and aggressively promoting one's own agenda. Enough said.

Withholding or Withdrawing Life Support

Some of the most common ethical dilemmas that will be encountered by spiritual leaders surround the issue of withholding or withdrawing life support. Life support includes a variety of mechanical and medicinal interventions that are able to sustain life for a length of time. A key component of life support is the ventilator, or breathing machine. A new era for health-care ethics began in the 1970s with the widespread availability of the ventilator. Patients could now be intubated and their bodily functions maintained by a machine that would breathe for them. Since that time paramedics in the field have been trained to use a combination of drugs and temporary intubation ("bagging" the patient by hand) to save many lives and get an individual in cardiac or respiratory arrest to the hospital, where the ventilator can be utilized to stabilize the patient during the diagnostic process and as life-saving medical procedures are set in motion. Resuscitation in the field by first-line responders is now a standard of care. In other words, if you were to have a heart attack, go into cardiac arrest, and become unconscious, it is standard procedure for the ambulance crew to shock your heart to start it beating, put a breathing tube into your lungs to protect your airway, and rush you to the hospital, where you would be put on a ventilator. And this is the case whether you actually died on the scene or if you have the potential to live!

I have seen medicines start the heart of someone who had died several minutes earlier. This procedure is followed even if one has a living will. Many people are brought to our hospitals today who are declared dead within minutes because their heart cannot sustain a rhythm. And at that time the life-support machines are finally removed and death is declared. If the family has arrived to wait for the medical team to do what they can do, they are faced with a decision regarding how aggressive the care team should be. If the patient is still alive but the condition is nonsurvivable, then aggressive treatment can be *with-*

held (the ventilator disconnected), and comfort care instituted until death comes. If the ER physician believes the patient will recover, then appropriate life-sustaining measures will be taken. If the patient's condition decays, the family may have to make the decision whether or not to *withdraw* support. At that time the ventilator may be disconnected, with the care plan changed to reflect comfort measures in anticipation of death. Whether a patient recovers or not, his or her family will never forget those moments of decision making when the physician asked them about aggressive heroic life-sustaining measures.

Louise faced a particularly difficult situation when her husband, Joe, had a cardiac arrest. Joe had been going to a cardiologist for several months and knew that his heart was weakening. He and Louise had spent several long conversations around the woodstove in their home, discussing his feelings and what to do if a heart attack occurred. He was emphatic that he did not want any of that "new surgery" or any other "experimental doctoring," which he felt was unnatural and only prolonged a death that was going to come anyway. Joe was a hard-nosed ex-Marine and prided himself on accepting the fact that life had a beginning and an end. He was willing to face his end and let it go at that. And, like many of his friends, he distrusted the medical profession, which he saw as a black hole gobbling up the financial resources of hardworking middle-class people. Louise loved her husband and respected his courage, but she also knew it would be hard for her to follow through with his wishes when the time came. The time came sooner than she thought it would.

When Joe went out to start the car one morning, he did not return for several minutes. She finally went to check on him and discovered he had collapsed in the driveway. He was breathing but could not speak. She ran to call 911. Ten minutes later, the medical helicopter landed right on the front lawn of their rural property, and Joe was taken to the hospital. In the ER the physician read Joe's chart information and noted that he had significant heart disease, with three of his cardiac arteries 95 percent occluded. From the minute Joe arrived, his heart rhythm was irregular and he "coded" twice in the first fifteen minutes. Both times he was quickly shocked to start his heart again. When Louise arrived at the ER she was told that he had been resuscitated, given meds to stabilize his heart rate, and had been placed on a ventilator. She immediately thought of her and Joe's conversations and told the ER physician that he did NOT want any life-sustaining treatment. She started crying and tearfully said, "I don't want my husband to die." On the other hand, she also made it clear that she did not want

Joe to wake up on the ventilator. The ER physician in the meantime had notified Joe's cardiologist, and he shortly arrived on the scene to evaluate Joe's condition. After a few minutes of consultation, the cardiologist reported to Louise that Joe would need to have a defibrillator implanted in order to keep his heart from stopping as a result of its chronic irregular rhythm. He also recommended immediate angioplasty and stent placement, although he knew that his patient had already declined those options. Louise was unwilling to authorize the procedure, because she knew that her husband would refuse the defibrillator if he were awake and capable of responding. The cardiologist spoke with Louise for thirty minutes, seeking to change her mind and arguing for the benefits of the procedures. She listened and cried openly as he passionately tried to convince her that Joe didn't need to die. After these agonizing moments Louise gave in and made the decision to allow the ventilator for a limited period of time, and Joe was transferred to the ICU.

The end of Joe's story is that he was taken off of the ventilator the following day, probably prematurely for adequate healing of his body (but at Louise's insistence), and transferred out of ICU to a room on the floor. He never did get much strength back, and his heart grew weaker every day with him sleeping most of the time. He died ten days after his emergency trip to the hospital. Louise spent each day with him and was devastated when he finally passed away. She had kept true to their agreements about his medical care, and for that she felt some satisfaction.

When Joe was taken to the hospital, Louise made several decisions that impacted the medical treatment he received. Ethically, she was able to make the decisions she did because of the principle of patient autonomy. Joe and Louise had the right to direct the care received, even if it was not in the best interests of Joe's health. For instance, some life-saving measures were withheld at his request, though there was no doubt they would have saved his life (angioplasty and stents for his blocked arteries). The cardiologist was definitely struggling personally with his ability to save Joe and being stymied by Louise. What he believed to be an ethical duty to save Joe's life conflicted with Louise's decision to follow Joe's wishes. So, again, the defibrillator implantation was another potential intervention withheld at Louise's request. Finally, she made the decision to withdraw the life-support systems in the ICU—including the ventilator—the next day. At that time there was no guarantee that Joe would die. But, as it turned out, he was just too weak and so continued his downhill slide. His is an example of the decision-making control that patients and families have in our modern medical system. And certainly also an illustration of just how common decisions to withhold or withdraw medical support are for patients and families dealing with cardiac or respiratory illnesses. Not all persons would agree with Joe and Louise's medical decisions. Most people would probably want everything possible done to save their life or the life of their spouse, but this is what makes for the interesting twists that result in ethical disagreements between patients, their families, and their medical caregivers.

Organ Donation

One of the conditions of participation in the Medicare/Medicaid program, upon which hospitals rely for the majority of their funding, mandates that when a death occurs in the hospital, next-of-kin be given the opportunity to make organ or tissue donation. The need is great, with over 70,000 individuals across our country waiting for a life-saving organ transplant. But when tragic circumstances occur and organ donation, with its multilayered personal issues, enters our life arena, new and subtle factors weigh upon us and often make the decision a hard one. Because death and grief are always a part of the organ donation equation, emotions run high, and everyone, including the medical staff, finds themselves in a crisis mode of operation.

One morning a fifty-five-year-old lady in otherwise good health was admitted to the hospital to receive treatment for an erratic heart rhythm. That afternoon she developed a headache and asked for a pain reliever before taking a nap. When she did not awaken after a little over an hour, her RN tried to arouse her, with no result. Frantically, tests were ordered and it was discovered that she had an aneurysm that had burst in her brain. The RN and every one of the staff involved with her care were shocked and devastated by this unforeseen turn of events. At 9:00 p.m. the neurologist was forced to call a family conference to let the three adult daughters know that their mother was brain-dead and on life support in the ICU. The intracranial bleeding had caused her brain to swell. All of this a mere six hours after being admitted to the hospital for what was thought to be an erratic heartbeat. The daughters were shaken and tearful as they asked questions about how this could have happened. Although everything had been done treatment-wise to protect the patient, given the information available when she was admitted, one daughter was openly angry at the turn events had taken and was critical of the hospital and staff. In anticipation that the family would need to be approached about organ donation, a spiritual-care support person was notified to be with the family. For this moment pretend that person is *you*. What issues would influence your approach to organ donation as you support these grieving daughters? Are there concerns about the patient's death? What role might the one daughter's anger play in the donation process?

Probably the first matter that would guide your approach as a spiritual-care support person for the daughters would be the sudden and unanticipated death of a recently healthy mother. There would no doubt be a lot of processing and remembering of the mother's life as they start to realize that, yes, her life is over. A natural response to this situation is for family members to want to give the dying loved one as many good moments as possible, which means protection from any undue pain. If organ donation is seen by the family as a painful surgery and, in effect, a mutilation process, then the likelihood of them agreeing to it is minute. As their support and advocate, you would be listening and hearing their grief and processing. It would be inappropriate for you to try to convince them to do the organ donation, especially if it seemed that they were adamantly protective of their mother's body.

A second issue might be the diagnosis of brain death. When a loved one is still breathing and looking quite alive, even though surrounded by invasive tubes and other medical apparatus, to convince oneself that the person is already dead sometimes goes against our natural thought processes. We hope that the person will still recover. And this is definitely the case when a sudden illness, as is the one in our example, takes a healthy person from life to death in such a short time period. It takes people longer than a day to grasp the significance of the loss and to adjust to the idea of death. Adjustment is a process and education is helpful as persons attempt to understand what has happened. A good pastoral intervention is to make sure families have a handout on brain death and what it means for the patient. These are usually available from hospital staff (an RN or preferably a chaplain). Interestingly enough, various surveys have shown that up to 70 percent of clergy disagree with brain death as a measure of true death. I suppose this comes from having religious difficulty with the notion that the spirit has left the body when the heart is still beating. Many cultures around the world have religious practices that attend to the body for several days after death because they believe the spirit takes time to leave the body. It is an important self-awareness for you to know *your* theological understanding of the spirit and body interaction before you find yourself as a patient advocate in an organ donation situation.

It has helped me, in my understanding of brain death, to think about the injury to the brain as so damaging that survival is impossible. The brain is not functioning and we don't do brain transplants. So the individual sustaining such a significant injury would have no hope of ever being well again. In addition, a brain death diagnosis means that there is no thinking, no pain, no sensation experienced by the patient. Therefore, death has in reality occurred, whether the heart is still beating or not. I believe that the human spirit goes immediately to heaven at the time the injury reaches that critical point, based on Jesus's words to the thief on the cross during the crucifixion: "Today you will be with me in paradise" (Luke 23:43). However, there are other points of view, and *your* point of view will be the important one when you are with a family in that situation as their spiritual care advocate.

Another impact on this family's processing of the organ donation decision was the one daughter's anger. If the anger were directed toward the hospital and its staff, the act of donation could be seen by her as benefiting the hospital (or at least following the hospital's desired outcome), and therefore psychological resistance might be present against letting the hospital "have its way." Even though hospitals receive no institutional or financial gain from the number of organ donations they participate in, I have seen families in anger attempt to "get back" at the hospital by refusing organ donation. If, as a Christian minister, you felt that saving lives through organ donation was of significant ethical weight to advocate for a donation in this instance, as the family's advocate your intervention might be to defuse the anger of the daughter by working with the chaplain or the RN to set up a family conference with the daughter and involved hospital staff. As earlier noted, many of the hospital staff were particularly upset by the patient's downturn in this instance. Sharing that information in a family conference is a powerful bridge-building and communication tool. The patient's RN was very compassionate toward the family and saddened by her death. Being able to communicate that compassion to the family could do much to defuse the daughter's anger.

A final ethical issue in donation that may enter the picture with a particularly educated family might be the profit-making direction that some organ procurement agencies have taken, or the movement toward buying and selling organs. Some exploitation of the bereaved, the poor, and the uninformed has no doubt occurred when organ donation is overseen by certain abject agencies. In general, however, the opportunity to impact lives in many positive ways by being involved in the organ donation process (including the saving of multiple lives through the participation of one donor) is a benefit far outweighing the burdens of the process. With all of these potentially volatile issues waiting in the background, organ donation is a definite concern in a death situation and poses a variety of ethical dilemmas for families.

Informed Consent and Truth Telling

The image we have of informed consent is sometimes focused only on that piece of paper we sign before undergoing a surgical procedure. What we usually remember from that form is the variety of scary complications, including the possibility of death, which the procedure may cause given the worst-case scenario. In actuality the purpose of informed consent is to involve the patient and family in the planning and direction of their individual medical treatment and care plan. It is a patient's right to be informed of the medical diagnosis/prognosis and of the prescribed course of action by the physician, and to be given adequate information to make informed decisions as treatment progresses. What information is important? Information typically shared by physicians or other medical professionals includes relevant treatment alternatives, the pros and cons (benefits and risks) of the treatment, the reason the decision needs to be made, and any uncertainties or inherent risks of the proposed intervention.[6] Ethical issues arise when patients are reluctant to ask questions or incompetent, or when physicians are too hurried or obstinate to explain procedures. Sometimes issues of truth telling enter the picture. This is a problem that has been around since the beginning of the practice of medicine. For instance:

> In the Hippocratic volume *Decorum,* physicians are cautioned to conceal most things from patients and to appear always cheerful and serene, so as to distract the patient's attention from what is happening. Throughout medieval and early modern times, the physician's role as authoritarian healer was emphasized, with little evident concern for truthful disclosure of information. . . . That is, clinicians may be tempted to hide, shade, or lie about clinical information because of the fear that it will upset the patient and be to his or her overall detriment.
>
> This fear takes many forms: that patients will misunderstand or exaggerate the importance of the information; that they will worry unnecessarily about something for which there is nothing to be done; or that

the information will cause psychological distress, depression, or even suicide.[7]

'As a patient's spiritual-care advocate, you will be in a position to ask questions of the medical caregivers and to *illuminate the truth* for family members who are distracted by concern for their loved one. Unfortunately, physicians are under increasing pressure from the sheer numbers of patients they have to treat, and so spending a length of time with any one family to answer their questions is sometimes avoided. Insistence is an important advocate quality. Be aggressive in asking for explanations and the meaning of medical terms.

Physicians usually will not directly lie, unless directed to by a family member threatening a lawsuit. Instead, information will be withheld, or there will be selective disclosure or omission of all the facts. Sometimes a non-response to a question is used as a method of concealment. It's the old "Oh, I didn't hear you" routine. Use of medical terminology to hide the truth is another common practice. Calling cancer a "growth" or a "neoplasm" is not a lie, but it is not giving the full picture to an upset patient hoping the lesion is benign. Red flags for the perceptive advocate might include such *patient characteristics* as being uneducated or intellectually slow, unlikable, disenfranchised, or exhibiting adverse health behaviors; the *type of information* as potentially upsetting, a serious diagnosis or prognosis, or information already told to other family members; or the *potential consequences* as evoking strong emotional reaction, likely to affect or change decision making, or effects on others.[8]

It is very common for family members to want to hide the truth of a new diagnosis or terminal diagnosis from someone they love. Reasons for not telling the truth are usually "She will be hysterical," or "He has to heal his body first, and then we can worry about the future," or "She has been treated for depression, and we don't want her to slip mentally," or "He will get angry and hostile, so let's wait until he leaves the hospital." Other excuses abound. A particularly difficult situation for a spiritual advocate is when a patient is dying and the family does not want the patient to know. Sometimes I have had a direct request from a loving husband or wife to *not* tell his or her spouse they were dying. What would you do? How would you handle this situation? I have always felt it important to inform dying patients that their time on earth is ending, and therefore I usually speak out in favor of having that opportunity to inform the patient. Prayer at a time like that has tremendous purpose and meaning.

The topical spread of ethical issues and dilemmas is nearly unending. We have examined in this short chapter only a few of the myriad of possibilities you will encounter. But with these in mind, let's turn now to an analysis of decision making itself. How are ethical principles applied in decision making, and what factors are helpful in forming a contemporary model for ethical decision making?

Notes

1. Ann Freeman Cook, Helena Hoas, and Jane Clare Joyner, "Ethics and the Rural Nurse: A Research Study of Problems, Values, and Needs," *Journal of Nursing Law* 7, no. 1 (2000): 44.

2. Jacques P. Thiroux, *Ethics: Theory and Practice,* 7th ed. (Upper Saddle River, NJ: Prentice Hall, 2001), 56.

3. Ibid., 60f.

4. Stanley J. Grenz, *The Moral Quest* (Downers Grove, IL: InterVarsity Press, 1997), 29.

5. I am indebted to Stanley Grenz for raising my awareness of this issue. See ibid.

6. Jeremy Sugarman, *Ethics in Primary Care* (New York: McGraw-Hill, Health Professions Division, 2000), 250.

7. Ibid., 133–34.

8. Ibid., 140.

7

A Decision-Making Model
for Ethical Dilemmas

Sometimes personal reflection upon *how* a decision is to be made is almost as important as the *final* decision. This is especially the case when no clear-cut biblical guidance applies to the ethical dilemma we face. There are many moral issues upon which scripture speaks definitively and gives the Christian guidance. But as we have seen, a decision to withdraw life support, make an organ donation, or withhold emergency treatment can be approached by our loved ones from completely different operational value systems, even though all may be from a committed Christian background. Other rationales enter our minds when deciding what Uncle Joe or Aunt Mary may have wanted done in a life-altering medical decision. So a model for ethical decision making is helpful and important as we ready ourselves as Christian leaders to be effective advocates and think about each individual case. But a model such as the one we will look at is no guarantee for finding the *right* answer. No model is a fail-safe formula in these tough situations. The only right answer is the one that fits with all the circumstances in the case. And, though this model is consistent with scripture, it can be utilized by people from many different faith backgrounds and denominations, or even those from a non-Christian background.

In addition, this model comes from a *facilitation* approach rather than an authoritarian approach. As we have seen in our study of Paul's letter to Philemon, taking an approach of coming alongside to walk with a person in compassionate respect and acceptance is more effective when dealing with sensitive issues than is an aggressive confrontation that tries to force a particular agenda upon someone. As Christian advocates, we must listen, clarify, ask questions, pray, and allow the Holy Spirit to bring the conviction of the best decision to the one facing the crisis, given the information he or she has at the time. It is an awesome and dreadful place to be in life when you are having to make the decision, but a blessing for those allowed to share it with you as a support and advocate.

The following decision-making model is based upon guidelines set out by the Society for Health and Human Values–Society for Bioethics Consultation Task Force on Standards for Bioethics Consultation, with some modification in terminology.[1] So as a model it is thoroughly medically based and would be recognized as such by physicians in your hospital. In a tough decision-making situation, any chaplain or social services staff would be an added help in walking with you as clergy through this process. To tackle an ethical dilemma, do the following:

1. Gather relevant information (for example, medical information, relevant facts, physician and family concerns, and a statement of the decision-making problem).
2. Clarify personal values and personal ethical position related to the case (verbalize operational value system, family traditions, personal wishes, autonomy issues, faith-based values, standards of care, and why they conflict in the case).
3. Clarify related normative issues and ethical principles (such as beneficence, nonmaleficence, autonomy, justice, informed consent, spiritual values, biblical principles, other ethical principles, law/legal issues, institutional policies—these norms will come from family, physicians, caregivers, and other persons involved in the case).
4. Help to identify a range of morally acceptable options within the patient context (generate alternatives and prioritize them with a view toward those consistent with named values). Make a decision.
5. Evaluate the decision made (weigh the burdens/benefits, consequences, and reengage in the decision-making process if the ethical dilemma is not resolved). Did the right thing happen?

Ethical decision making is really just a matter of gathering information, letting everyone verbalize what their gut-level concerns are in the case, adding important principles that apply from all involved persons, and then coming to the point of having to decide. Unfortunately, in many cases one cannot go back and change a medical decision once it is made. The consequences usually are permanent. But continual evaluation and "remaking" of the plan of care is a daily process in the treatment of patients. Nevertheless, the stakes are usually high. For instance, this next case example is especially difficult. After the facts of the case are given, as an illustration of how to analyze an ethical dilemma we will walk through the decision-making process following the steps above.

Case Study #1

Ron and June were both in their twenties, with no children, happily married, and enjoying their fifth year as a couple, when one night during dinner at a favorite restaurant Ron began choking on a piece of meat suddenly lodged in his throat. Though June attempted to dislodge the piece and called for help, Ron slipped into unconsciousness and eventual respiratory arrest. By the time the emergency medical team arrived and managed to get an airway established, Ron was clearly blue and affected by the lack of oxygen. After several days in the ICU, it was determined that Ron would have permanent and massive brain damage. He would never be able to feed himself, would never regain adult mental ability, and would need continual care for basic health needs. He wouldn't be able to speak, since all of the language areas of the brain had been affected by the lack of oxygen. He was able to open his eyes and communicate with some facial expressions and arm movements. Though she was devastated by the scope and devastating nature of her husband's injury, June determined to take care of Ron and to dedicate her life to that end for as long as he should live.

June became Ron's full-time caregiver. She gave up her job and received disability payments from Ron's Social Security, which allowed her to spend each day watching over him. She learned to read his moods and understand his ways of communication. Though he could give little back, he did smile at June when she touched his face to let her know she made him happy and that he loved her. They lived this hard but satisfying life together for many years. However, Ron's troubles were not over.

Nearly twenty years later Ron suddenly suffered a devastating stroke that landed him again in the ICU. The brain bleed caused additional damage, this time taking away what remained of his cognitive and neurological ability (according to the physicians), and requiring Ron to be on a ventilator for the rest of his life. According to his pulmonologist and neurologist, Ron would be unable to sustain this new level of physical need—with its attendant care—for very long and would die from an infection sometime soon. They encouraged June to withdraw the life-support measures and let Ron die naturally. The physicians were in agreement that they were prolonging Ron's death and causing undue suffering for him as he languished on the breathing machine in the ICU. June was having a difficult time thinking about letting Ron go. Then, after nearly three weeks in ICU, June noticed that Ron was responding to her with his familiar arm and eye communication. She realized he was certainly not the same as he had been prior to the stroke, but this change gave her hope that he was improving and raised her spirits. Unfortunately, the physicians did not see the same subtle communication that June saw. They believed her to be in denial of the fact that Ron was irreparably impaired. Several new consults were ordered, with each new physician agreeing that Ron had no mental ability and therefore no true quality of life. June would not listen. Her Christian background and hope that Ron was improving kept her from turning off the machines and giving up on Ron. In addition, she felt that God would take Ron when God's timing was right. She expressed to the doctors that she didn't want to be responsible for ending his life prematurely. Anger erupted on both sides on several occasions. June requested a hospital transfer. An ethics consultation was eventually called.

Case Analysis

1. Gather relevant information.

By the time the ethics consultation was called, each party was distrustful of the other, and displays of anger had made communication between them difficult. This alone provides an ethical problem. The decision-making problem in Ron's case ultimately has to do with his long-term care. The physicians wanted life support withdrawn, and Ron's wife wanted life support and long-term ventilator support continued indefinitely until Ron died of natural causes. She insisted that

Ron be transferred to a different hospital and therefore to different physicians who might care about his life and work to save it.

From the physicians' point of view, Ron medically had suffered a fatal stroke that had left his brain so significantly damaged that no rational processes would ever be a part of his experience again. He would never eat on his own. He would never breathe on his own. He would need continual drug monitoring and ventilator support for the rest of his life. He would never communicate. In effect, he would be a vegetable. He would surely die at this time if heroic measures were withdrawn. Medically, there was no intervention that could "make him well." And with the risk of infection, his long-term prognosis would be poor to nil. Certainly he would not have what would be considered anything close to a normal human life. Initial attempts at physician/family conferences were not received well. Anger was directed toward June for her denial and for possible self-serving financial greed, as she stood to gain from providing continued support for her husband. The physicians wanted support withdrawn and Ron to be allowed to die with dignity.

From June's point of view, Ron was showing signs of improvement. Communication was becoming possible. She had taken care of him for twenty years and could now see meaningful signs of improvement that were missed by the less-observant doctors. June had had several rounds of disagreements with her physicians, and she did not trust them any more. She experienced them as wanting to take her husband away from her. June said that she knew Ron would die someday, but that God would take him "when it is his time to go."

2. Clarify personal values and personal ethical positions related to the case.

The physicians acted out of the best of their professional standards of care. They expressed awareness of the financial and justice issues involved with providing heroic care in a futile life situation. They recognized the societal burden that would be borne if Ron utilized valuable scarce resources. They expressed great compassion toward Ron and June and the terrible turn events had taken; however, they were realistically aware that death would be inevitable for Ron and that to put him through more suffering would be a burden they felt unable in good conscience to bear. Accordingly, the principle of nonmaleficence (to do no harm) in Ron's case required that life support be withdrawn. Additional consults with other professional specialties had failed to reach a reasonable outcome. All the professionals had attempted to keep June well abreast of their opinions and followed good practices of informed consent with all procedures.

June approached Ron's crisis with a great personal and emotional investment. In addition to her Christian values that propound the sacredness of life and the sovereignty of God in matters of life and death, she might also have been fighting a hidden inward battle of guilt and grief. When Ron first choked on the meat, June was unable to rescue him or get help to him in time to prevent permanent disability and the resulting family tragedy. June certainly remembered this as a traumatic incident in her life. Though there was nothing more that she could have done, still she might have developed a mistaken feeling of guilt for her inability to save him. And over the length of twenty years, this guilt could have had the potential of becoming a deep-seated personality pathology. She was not truly guilty, but she might have believed otherwise. This loss of Ron's ability to function was also a significant life change for June. Such a drastic change could bring on a grief/loss cycle with which she may not have dealt adequately and which may have been complicated by Ron's continuing health problems and need for immediate caregiving. After all, she couldn't spend time dealing with *her* problems. She had to attend to Ron and his needs. The potential loss of Ron through real death at this point in time may have been more than June could cope with. It would be natural to seek to avoid Ron's death at all costs.

A final issue in June's life might have been a financial one coupled with an identity crisis. Since all of her time was invested with Ron's care, it would be a tremendous shock to have that end. Personality theory states that people will attempt to preserve their sense of identity at nearly all costs, and after twenty years, June's identity was in being Ron's caregiver. What would she do with her life should he leave her in death? And since she relied on his Social Security disability payments as her only source of income, his death could have affected her adversely financially, even to the point of losing her home. That is a lot of change!

In summary, June had issues of faith, of false guilt, of grief, of identity, and of financial loss should Ron die. Some of these may be so dreadful to her as to be buried beneath feelings of anger and mistrust. She has the patient's right as Ron's legal caregiver to seek alternative treatments of care. Through patient/family autonomy she has the right to direct the care of her husband, even to the point of disagreeing with physicians. This she does quite well.

3. Clarify related normative issues and principles.

The norms that have a bearing on the case include:

Beneficence/Nonmaleficence toward the patient. These principles focus upon "doing good" and "doing no harm" on the patient's behalf and seeking what is ultimately in the patient's best interests. Beneficence is grounded in compassion and biblical love for human beings. Sometimes, the "good" thing is to forgo technological intervention and let a patient die.

Autonomy and freedom of the individual or family. Autonomy is a fundamental cornerstone of American medicine and is recognized by physicians in all hospitals. It has to do with patient preferences of care and refusal of care that is in conflict with personal values or traditions. Autonomy allows a patient or family to request additional physicians, consults, or even a transfer to another hospital where their wishes can be carried out.

Professional duty and integrity. This is the ethical commitment of the medical profession and physicians to advocate for appropriate care in consultation with peers and other professional staff. Standards of care are followed with a view toward improving the health of members of society and enriching the long-term viability of health-care services. In Ron's situation, the physicians could not professionally recommend long-term treatment, given his physical challenges.

Respect for human dignity. This principle focuses upon protecting human dignity, allowing natural processes to take their course (in spite of technological intervention), the sacred nature of life and its inherent value, and a presumption toward saving and preserving life. In our case above, this norm is conflicted and is claimed by both the physicians and Ron's wife, June. The physicians claim respect for human dignity in the sense of wanting Ron to be allowed to die with dignity, and June claims respect for human dignity in the sense of her wanting to preserve Ron's life.

Institutional policies pertaining to this case would allow for Ron to be transferred to a medical center of June's choice. The withholding/withdrawal of life-support policy would allow the ventilator to be removed, given Ron's diagnosis, should June desire to end heroic measures on Ron's behalf. Relevant state law would allow withdrawal/withholding of life support given the terminal nature of Ron's illness.

*4. Identify a range of morally acceptable options, and make a
decision.*

Alternative 1: Follow the physicians' recommendations and withdraw life support; give comfort care until Ron dies
from natural causes.

Alternative 2: Maintain all aggressive support, stabilize Ron, and
transfer him to a long-term treatment center where
ventilator support is offered. In this alternative,
June would be forced to relocate, since no care centers in her city provide long-term patient ventilator
support.

Alternative 3: Transfer Ron immediately to a different medical center where June could feel comfortable that a "new
start" had been made and new physicians could be
involved with Ron's care and treatment. Finding such
a hospital might be difficult, since receiving physicians must be willing to accept Ron as a patient and
find cause to believe they will be of some use in bringing him to renewed health.

Decision: The decision made in this case was to transfer Ron
to an out-of-state, regional skilled care center offering
ventilator support. He remained in ICU another month
until he was able to travel by medical airline.

5. Evaluate the decision made.

Did the right thing happen? Ron's case was a particularly difficult
ethical dilemma for everyone involved. The physicians expressed their
disappointment that June was so upset with them, and yet to this day
they speak of Ron as representing the most difficult ethical case they
have encountered in their practice of medicine. Anger toward the
family is still an issue.

The futile nature of long-term care, the undue suffering that Ron
endured, and the ineffectual use of precious medical resources are the
concerns that were the fundamental stumbling blocks for the medical staff. Because Ron was transferred to a different medical center,
I have no knowledge of how his life went from this point on, nor of
how June dealt with his continued medical crisis. But that is not the
point for us.

What is important for us to recognize (in addition to the process of the decision-making model) is that an involved advocate may have been able to facilitate communication, get issues on the table, and defuse some of the distrust that developed between June and her physicians. Lest you think the physicians uncaring, you need to know that both of them were committed Christians and very involved in their own local churches. They were acting out of their own perspectives of compassion and care in how they treated Ron's medical crisis. In addition, June did have a local pastor with whom she was close and whom she consulted throughout this critical time period. But he was absent from the hospital scene! He did not help her in expressing her feelings to the physicians and, like many of us, probably felt it to be outside of his scope of ministry to get involved with advocacy. What we need are pastors and teachers who are equipped for medical ethics decision making and who are willing to be involved. I hope that will be you.

Case Study #2

A seventy-eight-year-old woman named Diane called her doctor after experiencing a tight feeling in her chest accompanied by pressure and shortness of breath. Examination in the ER confirmed that she had unstable angina pectoris. Because with this heart condition she was at risk for a potentially fatal arterial blockage, the doctor's recommendation was that she be hospitalized immediately and that tests be ordered to determine the extent of the blockage. At this point Diane balked and wanted to return home. She started to hurriedly gather her things while explaining to the staff that she had recently experienced the "hospital's bureaucracy" when her husband, Sam, died. She didn't want the same thing to happen to her.

As she told the story, Sam had talked many times about the end of his life and not wanting to have all the tubes and interventions that would keep him alive past his time to go. Sam was very practical and was appalled by the waste of money that often happens when medical people "start up with their incessant tests." Sam had terminal lung cancer and had been to the doctor several times. During one hospitalization several months earlier, Sam had been intubated by a doctor after making it clear to the doctor that he didn't agree with the procedure. Although he responded to the treatment, after getting off the ventilator he stated emphatically, "I will sue anyone who puts me on a machine like that again." Diane said that he went home after that hospital visit but was in poor health and continued to decline in strength and in his ability to navigate around the house. When he collapsed again at home on the day of his death, Diane called their physician, frantically saying, "The EMTs have started doing CPR, and they won't stop." She had repeatedly asked the ambulance crew to cease their efforts to save Sam and to let him die. But they would not stop and ended up transporting Sam to the hospital. Sam died shortly after arriving at the ER.

With this episode framing Diane's medical understanding, it is no wonder that when the ER doctor attempted to convince her that she needed to stay for diagnostic tests and emphasized that her life might be endangered should she not treat her illness, she emphatically replied, "I don't want to be in the hospital where they have all those machines. I don't want any tests or surgery. I've had a good life and am not afraid to die. I will be happy to join Sam. I miss him so much." She refused to be hospitalized and, with the staff still pleading for her to reconsider, left the ER "against medical advice" (AMA).

Case Analysis

1. Gather relevant information.

Diane had been diagnosed with unstable angina pectoris, which often indicates an occlusion of a coronary artery. Standard protocol would be to admit her to the hospital and run several tests to determine the seriousness of the blockage. She expressed some distrust of the doctor and hospital bureaucracy based upon the experience of her spouse, who was hospitalized several times previous to his death. During those admissions his personal wishes regarding end-of-life care and extent of treatment were not taken seriously by a doctor. Because of this, Diane refused to be admitted or even to listen to explanations by the ER staff. In addition she said that she had "lived a good life" and was ready to be with Sam. The decision-making problem had to do with the feelings of the ER staff, who were concerned about the potential risk to Diane's life and the possible responsibility to protect her life, versus Diane's decision to bear the consequences of her illness, leave the ER without treatment, and risk further physical injury or death.

2. Clarify personal values and personal ethical positions related to the case.

The ER staff and doctor, as professional caregivers, valued Diane's life and knew that she would receive the help she needed through appropriate interventions and would be given the possibility of living a happy and productive life for years to come. They were no doubt afraid that Diane might be personally unaware of the seriousness of her illness and the finality of death should a critical blockage occur. They may have questioned whether Diane was clinically depressed. She would be at risk for depression, given the fact that her husband of many years recently died. Grief often is a precursor to depression. Does she feel hopeless and alone? Is she afraid of the future if she has to live it by herself? If depression is an issue, is she competent to make a life-and-death decision like leaving the hospital AMA? Should she receive a mental-health evaluation? In addition, she had no family or friends at the hospital to support her or give needed advice. The ER staff felt uncomfortable just letting her go home.

Diane knew that she had a heart problem, but she was seventy-eight years old and accepted the fact that her life was coming to an end. She had been very much affected by what she saw as excessive medical intervention in her husband's final days. She felt that the hospital personnel were arrogant and not willing to listen. She experienced their jumping to the conclusion that she needed hospitalization as a lack of respect toward her and her personal wishes. If they jumped at admitting her so quickly, they might also intubate *her* later without her permission, and then who knew what else! She might have been oversensitive to their advances, but after all, they didn't listen when her husband was hospitalized. Diane had always been an independent lady, and that was one area of her life that she could still hold to now that her husband was gone. Diane was still grieving the loss of Sam and often wished she could die to be with him. She didn't see this as depression but just as a reality of life. It would be a lot lonelier in the coming months. She was ready to die if God wanted to take her.

The ethical dilemma in this case is one of patient autonomy and refusal of treatment versus beneficence and physician responsibility to act in the best interests of the patient. Patient competency may be an issue, as well as the value of trust and respect in a patient/physician relationship.

3. Clarify related normative issues and ethical principles.

Beneficence (the duty to do good) is a physician's principal motivation for acting in the best interests of the patient and in protecting a patient's health and saving a life. The physician and ER staff feel this ethical principle as a primary reason they are doing the work that they are.

Patient autonomy is an ethical principle allowing individual freedom in refusing medical treatment, even if that refusal may be detrimental to health or a cause of death. Diane has the personal right to stay at home and allow natural physical processes to take their course. She is an individual moral agent and bears individual responsibility for her life.

Informed consent requires that a patient be given information needed to make an intelligent decision regarding treatment or plan of care. The ER physician and staff were able to give Diane enough information regarding her diagnosis to relieve of them of the legal responsibility of her life. She was able to verbalize to them that she understood the risk she was taking in leaving the medical center AMA. In all aspects she demonstrated that she was a competent adult making a competent decision.

Respect as an ethical principle is founded on the inherent value of each person in a relationship. A patient/physician relationship based on respect leads to a shared decision-making approach that values the input of professional recommendations, as well as individual patient desires. Trust in the relationship is a result of mutual respect. Diane did not feel valued by the physician or staff and therefore experienced a lack of trust. Law does not require admission for hospital treatment.

4. Help to identify a range of morally acceptable options, and make a decision.

Alternative 1:   The ER physician and staff had no choice but to let Diane go home, even though it rubbed against their inclination to help her with her medical problem. There were no legal grounds for keeping her. The one choice they had would be *how* to deal with her after she left the hospital. Appropriate follow-up by Diane's primary physician would be good medical practice and a demonstration of compassionate care. The ER staff might also initiate a dialogue regarding staff strategies to rebuild trust in patients who have had negative hospital experiences in the past.

Decision: Diane was allowed to leave the hospital, against medical advice.

5. Evaluate the decision made.

The value of this relatively simple ethical dilemma is found in recognizing the human values that often come to the forefront in medical treatment. There was a definite disagreement and conflict between Diane and her caregivers based upon perceived excesses in medical treatment received by Sam prior to his death. The distrust she developed as a result probably affected the length of her own life. Our individual feelings and compassion for Diane are brought to the surface as we hear her story and begin to understand her feelings about how she wants to die and her personal wishes in end-of-life care. As observers we naturally want her to take care of herself and receive the treatment that will extend her life. She, on the other hand, has a totally different agenda based upon personal independence, financial responsibility, and love for her departed spouse. Her decision to leave AMA was the right one for her. The opportunity for the ER staff to dialogue about this case was an important outcome of the dilemma. This is the sort of patient issue that staff will take home and dwell upon, not feeling very good about how things developed or were resolved. Diane's case is a good example of an ethical issue that is experienced by caregivers as significant but in reality is a legitimate patient decision.

If Diane had a spiritual advocate with whom she could have consulted during this crisis, that person could have perhaps been a mediator between the ER staff and herself. Diane's anger after Sam's experience could have been put on the table by the advocate, and her concerns about excessive treatment outlined and documented so that her specific wishes for care would be followed. That pastor, elder, or Christian support person could have allayed the fears of the staff regarding Diane's state of mind and perhaps have helped in defusing Diane's fears of the hospital. In the best case, perhaps Diane could have been given alternative options for cardiac treatment that may have worked to raise the quality of her life until it was God's time to take her.

Conclusion

An ethical dilemma is experienced as something that strikes us as being "abnormal" or "not right" when viewed from the perspective of our own operational value systems. When we get the feeling that something "seems wrong" and can verbalize what bothers us in a decision-making process, then we are on the way to a better self-understanding of issues. To resolve an ethical dilemma we follow a process of gathering information, verbalizing personal values, and interacting with ethical principles and moral norms important to those involved, and we finally make the best decision possible. A model such as this one only helps in the process of analyzing a dilemma. Often the decision is still a very difficult one. But this is also where the spiritual strength of a relationship with God can make a big difference in a person's life.

Notes

1. Mark P. Aulisio, Robert M. Arnold, and Stuart J. Younger, "Health Care Ethics Consultation: Nature, Goals, and Competencies," *Annals of Internal Medicine* 133, no. 1 (July 2000): 61.

8

Christian Distinctives in Facing Ethical Dilemmas

A person who has made a Christian commitment is a "new creation" (2 Cor. 5:17) and has had his or her life philosophy radically changed by the message of the good news of Jesus Christ. For to accept Jesus as Lord means to accept the truth about his messianic identity, his miraculous birth, his authoritative teaching and miracles of healing, his death on the cross according to God's purposes in atonement for our sin, and his bodily resurrection to new life beyond the grave. With all this as a foundation of personal belief, the facing of a particular ethical dilemma in the context of a modern medical center takes on different meanings and brings to the fore different concerns and issues of faith for the follower of Jesus. Our understanding of God's love and care for his people permeates all that we encounter in the hospital, including speaking to physicians and other members of the care team about making medical decisions. We do not tread this ground alone. We walk by faith and not by sight. And we trust in God's intervention among us.

There is a wide range of theological beliefs and doctrines that inform the Christian when it comes to facing ethical dilemmas. Only a few of the many will be discussed in this chapter. But it is hoped that these will inspire further reflection and encourage those who are Christ's own to remember the things we hold to be true.

The Bible Is God's Gift of Truth

Basic to the teaching of Christianity is the truth that the one Creator God revealed himself to people through history, the prophets, the coming of his Son, and the gift of the written Word of God. The Bible is an indispensable resource for Christians seeking to find their way through a complex and often confusing life, and it is the first important Christian distinctive when medical decision making is at hand. Christians trust the Bible and read it for guidance when matters of God's will need to be discerned. In these matters the Bible is by God's design sufficient as a rule of Christian practice and faith but certainly not exhaustive in its scope of decision-making subject matter. It does not address all the medical decisions that we will be forced to deal with in our lives. There were no modern hospitals offering open-heart surgery, organ donation, or tube feedings in Jesus's day. But the Bible does show us "the mind of God," and when we immerse ourselves in its pages, we will learn to think and reflect according to God's pattern of decision making.

When Moses spoke to the people of Israel on the threshold of entering the Promised Land and reminded them of God's mighty acts in bringing them out of Egypt, he exhorted them to remember God's words and to have them upon their hearts.

> Acknowledge and take to heart this day that the LORD is God in heaven above and on the earth below. There is no other. Keep his decrees and commands, which I am giving to you today, so that it may go well with you and your children after you and that you may live long in the land the LORD your God gives you for all time.
>
> Deuteronomy 4:39–40

> Hear, O Israel: The LORD our God, the LORD is one. Love the LORD your God with all your heart and with all your soul and with all your strength. These commandments that I give you today are to be upon your hearts. Impress them on your children. Talk about them when you sit at home and when you walk along the road, when you lie down and when you get up. Tie them as symbols on your hands and bind them on your foreheads. Write them on the doorframes of your houses and on your gates. . . . The LORD commanded us to obey all these decrees and to fear

the Lord our God so that we might always prosper and be kept alive, as is the case today.

Deuteronomy 6:4–9, 24

It is important to note that the blessing associated with remembering God's words is one that carries over into our health and wellness. Moses told God's people to keep his words with the promise "that it may go well with you and your children after you and that you may live long in the land. . . ." So it is that the reading of the Bible is commanded for Christians and brings the promise of long life as we learn to think God's thoughts.

The Spirit of God also speaks through the pages of the Bible. The apostle Paul wrote these words concerning the inspiration of the Bible: "All Scripture is God-breathed and is useful for teaching, rebuking, correcting and training in righteousness, so that the man of God may be thoroughly equipped for every good work" (2 Tim. 3:16–17). In addition, Jesus told his disciples: "The words I have spoken to you are spirit and they are life" (John 6:63).

We must not forget that God guides our thinking and our imaginations through the reading of the Bible and by the working of his Spirit. When Christians come to the Bible within the context of their own problems and pressing concerns, God speaks truth to them through the message written long ago but alive for them today. It happens as a dynamic Spirit-led *hearing* of God's Word that illuminates the life situation of the reader. The Holy Spirit (according to Jesus) was sent to enliven the truth of the Bible and to "*teach you all things*" (John 14:26). The work of the Spirit brings ancient texts and contexts into contemporary life situations and applies them as truth to the lives of God's people who are seeking his guidance.

When faced with a hard medical decision, Christians will turn for guidance to the Bible as their first source of help. They will search the scriptures for ethical principles and moral teachings that bear upon the decision at hand. In doing so they are placing their lives under the authority of the Lord God and seeking his will in their lives and his purpose for the future. As a spiritual advocate you can be aware of the importance of the Bible both in decision making and as a source of strength and comfort. Families will often not have a Bible with them if they come to the hospital suddenly to respond to a crisis. You can know that hospitals will have Bibles available—if not in plain sight, then at least in the unit (ER, ICU, nursing floors). Don't hesitate to ask for a Bible from any of the nursing or chaplain staff. And then don't hesitate to minister to the family by reading passages that remind the family of God's care and concern, God's presence, and God's sovereignty in times of trouble. In my experience, even seasoned pastors often don't think about the ministry of God's Word when terrible tragedies have occurred. And yet a few appropriate scriptures read in times of fear or uncertainty make a big difference to a patient or family in crisis.

Knowledge of the Heart

Closely related to the illumination of the scriptures in the life of the believer is the even deeper illumination of the heart that comes hand in hand with a relationship to God. When Nicodemus asked Jesus about the Savior's relationship with God, Jesus responded by saying that "no one can see the kingdom of God unless he is born again." And when Nicodemus didn't understand, Jesus continued: "I tell you the truth, no one can enter the kingdom of God unless he is born of water and the Spirit" (John 3:3, 5). Jesus taught that understanding of "heavenly things" comes through being born of the Spirit (John 3:12–15). Christians believe that a miracle of regeneration occurs when a person believes Jesus and accepts him as Lord and Savior. At that time the Holy Spirit enters and makes the new believer a child of God through forgiveness of sins and the impartation of the righteousness of God. The apostle Paul wrote of this change when he addressed the church at Corinth:

> Therefore, if anyone is in Christ, he is a new creation; the old has gone, the new has come.
>
> 2 Corinthians 5:17

Part of the newness has to do with the renewal of the mind and heart, so that a spiritual comprehension is bestowed that previously was unavailable to the individual. Paul speaks of this in his writings to the Romans:

> Do not conform any longer to the pattern of this world, but be transformed by the renewing of your mind. Then you will be able to test and approve what God's will is—his good, pleasing and perfect will.
>
> Romans 12:2

The Bible speaks of the reality of spiritual blindness prior to a relationship with God.

> The god of this age has blinded the minds of unbelievers, so that they cannot see the light of the gospel of the glory of Christ, who is the image of God.
>
> 2 Corinthians 4:4

On the other hand, someone who is in a personal relationship with God in Christ has had his or her eyes opened to spiritual truth and to moral knowledge in a way that gives special insight to life situations and life problems. A Christian worldview has been gifted to them by the Spirit.

Tristram Engelhardt relates this unique heart knowledge, which is part of the Christian experience, to the choice to love God and says that it affects ethical reasoning:

> We must answer the command to love God. As we respond to that command, we are transformed by God. God acts to change those who turn to Him as they cooperate with God Who transforms them. The moral law within, the ability to love God and turn to God and to others in love, makes possible a personal response to God, and leads to the acquisition of moral, including bioethical, knowledge. Again, the moral law that is at the basis of traditional Christian bioethics is not a set of rules separate from or over against the persons who should obey them—it is part of them and properly their way of life. The moral law is integral to our turning in full love to God.[1]

So this heart knowledge can lead a Christian in the midst of a difficult ethical dilemma to discover special insights into the decision-making process. The insights might concern personal wishes of the patient or understandings regarding the processes of healing that will take place. Moral knowledge brings visceral understandings of things patently wrong or of things occurring in the process of decision making that must be God's will. Sometimes it is a perception of mysteries or simply a motivation by the Spirit for the Christian to walk in faith. St. Isaac of Syria, a church father, writes about spiritual knowledge as being related to fear of God:

> Natural knowledge, which is the discernment of good and evil implanted in our nature by God, persuades us that we must believe in God, the Author of all. Faith produces fear in us, and fear compels us to repent

and to set ourselves to work. And thus man is given spiritual knowledge, which is the perception of mysteries, and this perception engenders the faith of true divine wisdom. Spiritual knowledge is not, however, thus simply begotten of mere faith alone; but faith begets the fear of God, and when we begin to act from the fear of God, then out of the steady action of the fear of God, spiritual knowledge is born, just as Saint John Chrysostom has said, "For when a man acquires a will that conforms to the fear of God and to right thinking, he quickly receives the revelation of hidden things." And by "revelation of hidden things" he means spiritual knowledge.[2]

To someone without a Christian commitment or belief, this idea of spiritual knowledge may seem silly or even foolhardy. In the context of the modern medical center, where a variety of sophisticated technology is available, and standards of care demand utilization of interventions that *might* be questioned by someone employing heart knowledge of the Christian way for a particular patient, the possibility for disagreements and ethical disparities is real.

An illustration is given us in Numbers 21 in the account of the bronze snake put up on a pole by Moses. During the time in the wilderness after the escape from Egypt, the people of Israel were suddenly assaulted by a large number of venomous snakes. The snakes bit the people, many of whom died. In response to this crisis, God told Moses: "Make a snake and put it up on a pole; anyone who is bitten can look at it and live" (v. 8). The account ends with Moses obeying God, erecting the snake, with the result that "when anyone was bitten by a snake and looked at the bronze snake, he lived" (v. 9). The crucial fact of this account is that the people needed only to *look* at the snake on the pole to be cured. This is in stark contrast to normal modern medicinal practice. The people were not instructed to inhibit the flow of the poison, nor to follow any other process to treat the wound. They were not told to make any ointments or to fight the infection in any way. They *were* told by implication to cease from normal human remedies and to turn to God's remedy only, which was to look at the snake on the pole. This was no doubt very hard for them, since looking up at the snake would have taken their eyes from the continual patrolling they were having to do to keep themselves from being bitten by meandering snakes on the ground! This commandment by God would have been considered foolhardy by the medical practitioners of the day, yet was a word from God to specifically mitigate the crisis at hand. So too will modern medical practitioners be baffled by certain family requests of Christians relying upon knowledge of the heart that is guided by the present and living Spirit of God.

A recent example comes to mind of a young mother who was dying from cancer. The medical staff were certain that she only had a few weeks left and that she should prepare her family, say her good-byes, and face her coming death with openness and acceptance. Yet this mother declined hospice support, told the staff that she knew she would not die yet, and continued to pray and look forward to being well again. The physician and all her nurses came to the conclusion that she was in great denial. To her doctor's and nurses' surprise she rallied physically, went home, and continued to thrive beyond the medical expectations of her particular disease. When asked by others about her positive attitude, she just said, "I knew that it was not my time yet. God still had something for me to do." So it goes with heart knowledge.

In the midst of similar situations where medical staff appear to be at odds with a patient's understanding, it is the role of the spiritual advocate to support the patient—and her or his family—in their particular commitments of faith and heart. Physicians will respect the wishes of the patient and family even if that goes against their personal or professional beliefs *if* they can understand the patient's rationale or philosophy. Sometimes the advocate needs only to be one who is able to communicate exactly where the patient or family is coming from, and then perhaps interpret from a faith perspective why they have come to that place in their commitments. The clarifying of values and beliefs is a very common role of the spiritual advocate.

Spiritual Realities: Miracles, Angels, Evil

Christianity began with miracles. Miracles and the existence of spiritual realities such as God's supernatural healing power, angels as messengers and protectors of God's people, and the working of Satan and powers of evil are part of the traditional Christian worldview. As a Christian enters the modern hospital, there is a mixing in his or her personal experience of the scientific and technological sophistication of modern medical practice with the understanding of a spiritual reality that is unseen and yet affects life and health outcomes at least as dramatically as a physician's correct diagnosis and treatment. The importance of scientific explanations is not denied by the Christian patient, but a wider perspective that includes spiritual warfare and

God's intervention in the affairs of health and wholeness is also at the forefront of the Christian's thinking. This is often not understood by secularly oriented medical staff or physicians who approach life and healing with a less than holistic understanding of human existence.

As a spiritual leader, pastor, or elder walking with patients or families, each contact with them provides a demonstrable witness to the reality of the omnipotence, compassion, and presence of God in the context of suffering and illness. Prayer is often a central focus during times of fear and uncertainty. In situations in which a loved one is in imminent danger and life is threatened—such as in the ER after a sudden accident or after a cardiac/respiratory arrest—families will pray for a miracle and seek God's direct intervention on behalf of the patient. To call upon the God of Abraham, Isaac, and Jacob in the name of Jesus Christ to perform a mighty act of healing and restoration on behalf of the one they love is a common Christian response of faith. And many times the prayer of faith brings answers from a loving God who hears the cries of his people.

A miracle can be defined as a supernatural working of God that cannot be explained by scientific or natural causes. Jesus Christ showed great compassion and love toward persons who suffered from leprosy, blindness, hemorrhaging, and paralysis, among many others. His ministry was marked by miracles of healing and the doing of miraculous signs among the people who came to him. He never healed for selfish purposes or for personal popularity, but instead to bring glory to God his Father and to demonstrate his revelatory authority and role as God's Son. Healing in the name of Jesus continued after the resurrection in the ministry of the apostles in the Book of Acts and in the ministry of the Christian church from the first century to the present. One cannot read the Gospels or the New Testament without noticing the miraculous interventions of God in the lives of his people.

One of the joys of being a hospital chaplain is the continual exposure to examples of modern-day miracles and testimonies from God's people of healings and answered prayer in their lives. I've observed what I considered miracles in areas such as the medically unexplained recovery from a terminal illness, seeming changes in radiology test results (for instance, cancer diagnosis), unexplained cessation of physical signs or progression of a disease, and answered prayer in a variety of critical medical situations.

Of course, there are many times that a miracle is desired by a patient or family and one is not granted. The Christian pastor or advocate is often in the position of being a person of faith *and* being a person in touch with medical facts at the same time and in a way that is often difficult for the patient or family as they are trying to cope with the medical crisis of their loved one. A pastoral advocate who continually prays for a miracle without recognizing that our frail human bodies will die and are meant to die can be a hindrance to the faith of the person under his or her care. Sometimes we need to affirm God's presence in the crisis even though the outcome might be tragic. Helping a family member or patient understand God's love and presence when the worst seems to be happening is perhaps one of the greatest gifts of faith we can facilitate.

Angels are spiritual beings also prevalent in the Bible. Christian people throughout the ages have had visitations from angels that have, among other things, provided hope and assurance of God's protection during critical illnesses. Angelic visitations are most common among persons approaching death, but others in various circumstances have also seen angels. They are another reminder of the existence of spiritual realities and unseen spiritual activity that is continually taking place among us.

Angels are beings created by God for four reasons: to surround his throne with praise, to carry out spiritual acts, to be his messengers, and to protect his people. Many people believe they have been assigned a guardian angel. Christian patients in hospitals will place figures of angels by their bedside and wear pins on their gowns as reminders of God's protection and presence. Theologian Millard Erickson describes the appearance of angels with the following:

> In most cases angels are not seen. The Lord had to open the eyes of Balaam before he could see the angel standing in his way (Num. 22:31). Elisha prayed that the Lord would open the eyes of his servant; then the young man saw that the mountain was full of horses and chariots of fire round about Elisha (2 Kings 6:17). When angels are seen, they ordinarily have a manlike appearance, so that they may well be mistaken for men (Gen. 18:2, 16, 22; 19:1, 5, 10, 12, 15, 16; Judg. 13:6; Mark 16:5; Luke 24:4). Sometimes the glory of the Lord shines from them (Luke 2:9; 9:26). And they are sometimes seen to be wearing white clothing of brilliant appearance. . . . Note how Matthew describes the angel of the Lord who rolled the stone from Jesus' sepulchre: "His appearance was like lightning, and his raiment white as snow" (Matt. 28:3; cf. Ezek. 1:13; Dan. 10:6; Rev. 1:14 and 19:12).[3]

Angels are involved in ministering to spiritual needs as God directs. They are also involved in unseen spiritual struggles.

Christians understand that a cosmic battle is ongoing in the spiritual realm for the salvation of persons' souls. Angels and their fallen counterparts, demons, are in spiritual conflict. Paul writes:

> For our struggle is not against flesh and blood, but against the rulers, against the authorities, against the powers of this dark world and against the spiritual forces of evil in the heavenly realms.
>
> Ephesians 6:12

The chief of the demons goes by many names, including: the Evil One, the Devil, Satan, Adversary, Deceiver, Accuser, Beelzebub, Great Dragon, Father of Lies, and Murderer. The Evil One (along with his demons) continually works to oppose God and Jesus Christ, and his primary purpose is to deceive and destroy. Demon possession was common during the ministry of Jesus in the New Testament, and Jesus's healings were many times linked with exorcism and casting out demons. This reminds Christians that some illnesses may be connected with a spiritual battle and/or may have a spiritual cause at their source. Christians will ask themselves questions, when faced with illness or death, concerning these spiritual realities and will pray for God's intervention and protection as important decisions are made regarding patient treatment and care.

Death Is Not the End of Life

Christians have a strength in facing death that is uncommon in our secular society. Because Jesus's tomb was found empty three days after his death, his disciples became changed men and preached everywhere the message of resurrection—a message that spread like wildfire throughout the known world at that time and even in this day has continued to bring the reality of "life after life" to people afraid of dying. Jesus appeared many times to his disciples and friends, including to a group of 500 at one time, as a witness to the truth of his resurrection from the dead. Jesus proved himself to be the Alpha and the Omega, the Author of salvation, and the guarantor of eternal life. That life is a gift to his followers and will be recognized by all at the end of time, when the consummation of all things takes place. As John wrote in the Book of Revelation:

> Then I saw a new heaven and a new earth, for the first heaven and the first earth had passed away, and there was no longer any sea. I saw the

Holy City, the new Jerusalem, coming down out of heaven from God, prepared as a bride beautifully dressed for her husband. And I heard a loud voice from the throne saying, "Now the dwelling of God is with men, and he will live with them. They will be his people, and God Himself will be with them and be their God. He will wipe every tear from their eyes. There will be no more death or mourning or crying or pain, for the old order of things has passed away." He who was seated on the throne said, "I am making everything new!" Then he said, "Write this down, for these words are trustworthy and true."

Revelation 21:1–5

A wonderful strength and hope is enjoyed by Christians who realize that life in this world is moving toward a climax that will include for them a reunion with their Lord and friend Jesus Christ in a new city where God himself will be present and be its light (Rev. 22:5). Christians view themselves therefore as pilgrims in this world and as citizens of heaven.

The apostle Paul wrote of this heavenly citizenship in his letter to the Philippians:

But our citizenship is in heaven. And we eagerly await a Savior from there, the Lord Jesus Christ, who, by the power that enables him to bring everything under His control, will transform our lowly bodies so that they will be like his glorious body.

Philippians 3:20–21

Since our true citizenship is held in heaven, our journey in this life is only transitional, in a sense, with our primary motivation being to reach our goal—our homeland—in heaven.

If we "seek first the Kingdom of heaven," argued Jonathan Edwards in a sermon on Christ the pilgrim, then we have become pilgrims. "He that is on a journey, seeks the place he is journeying to. We ought above all things to desire a heavenly happiness: to go to be . . . with God, and dwell with Jesus Christ." What the pilgrim passes *en route* must be viewed as transient, "so we should enjoy heaven then rather than earthly things." We should travel in a state of self-denial, free from the burdens and temptations of life. "All other concerns of life ought to be entirely subordinate to this," he adds.[4]

Christians have a perspective concerning death that gives them a different approach to end-of-life decision making. This earthly life does not need to be preserved at all costs.

Tristram Engelhardt writes the following concerning our society's distorted views on valuing the postponement of death:

> If one does not know that each of our deaths leads to resurrection and final judgment, then the postponement of death can take on a dominating and distorting importance. . . . Because medicine has the power effectively to relieve much suffering and often postpone death, medicine has been able to claim immense social, political, and economic attention and resources. It is for this reason among others that medical centers have taken on the cultural roles that cathedrals once claimed in the West. Medicine has become a cardinal focus of cultural investment and energy. . . . Medical centers are now the place where many, if not most, seek to resolve the problems of their sexuality, suffering, dying, and death. . . . Against this dominating vision of medicine, Christianity offers a radical reorientation. This life is not all there is. Full meaning is to be found beyond death, and therefore medicine is not the art most needed for a healthy life.[5]

Since ultimate meaning and purpose in life is to be found "beyond death," Christians will have different priorities when it comes to heroic and aggressive measures to sustain life, or in dealing with pain management, or in making decisions on withholding/withdrawing treatment. "Christians have traditionally understood that they may engage in medical interventions as long as these do not impede the spiritual life. There is also the recognition that medicine should not be used if it significantly distracts from our life of prayer or brings us to being obsessed with preserving this life."[6] If medicine takes this role, it becomes an idol—in the Christian view—and distracts from the "pursuit of the Kingdom."[7]

The proper goal of life and our human pilgrimage is holiness. An individual's spiritual journey is of higher significance than what may or may not be happening strictly to the body. Medical center physicians are concerned with the health of the body, whereas Christians are concerned with the health of the spirit. Interventions to sustain life may be very important in a futile situation, given this Christian perspective, if the patient has not had time to repent of sin or to be baptized as a ritual of Christian passage. Or, in another example, the giving of adequate pain medicine to control intractable pain may be less than desirable for the Christian if it renders him or her unable to pray consciously and to receive the sacraments of the church. Engelhardt states:

Patients who find themselves still focused simply on pursuing whatever treatment will increase the quality of the life left to them or their dignity in dying, instead of focusing on entering into pious and prayerful relationship with God, should if morally and medically possible be treated until they face their finitude and turn to the Kingdom of Heaven. If at the end of life a patient is still engaged in this world rather than turning to God, further treatment should be encouraged in the hope that the patient will in repentance turn to God.[8]

Ultimately, life-beyond-this-life is to be the locus of attention for caregivers of the hospitalized Christian. Spiritual values in situations of mortality supersede merely physical care.

Once again, the spiritual leader and advocate can be the one to help the patient's family remember their spiritual commitments during a time when they may be unable to think clearly or may be distracted by fear and concerns of loss. Raising theological issues and commitments of faith to the verbal level is sometimes all that is needed to spark a family's thought process. Then the issues can be discussed with the medical center staff and the patient's physician to bring the care plan into harmony with family or patient wishes. The physician, of course, is going to want to hear the patient's family make the care plan requests. The words of the family pastor requesting changes on the family's behalf will not be well received. But such is the nature of the subtle advocacy role of the spiritual leader.

We Are Not Alone

One of the most encouraging of Christian beliefs is that we don't walk through this life by ourselves. We belong to the Father and to brothers and sisters in him who provide support when times get difficult and are available for us to lean on as life's load gets heavy. The support is actually twofold and comes through the inward presence of the Spirit of God and through the outward presence of the people of God.

The Holy Spirit is present inwardly in the life of every Christian who names Jesus as Lord (Rom. 8:9). He is the Third Person of the Trinity and was sent by Jesus to be our Comforter after Jesus ascended to the Father. The Spirit is truly Emmanuel "God with us" in Christ's absence. It is a wonderful gift from God to the Christian to have a "presence" with us who keeps us from being alone. This inward presence of the Spirit has several roles. A major role of the Holy Spirit is that of a counselor:

to illuminate us, to lead us to the truth, and to teach us what is needed for wisdom in specific life situations. Before he left them, Jesus spoke to his disciples about the role of the Holy Spirit:

> And I will ask the Father, and he will give you another Counselor to be with you forever—the Spirit of truth. The world cannot accept him, because it neither sees him nor knows him. But you know him, for he lives with you and will be in you.
>
> John 14:16–17

> But the Counselor, the Holy Spirit, whom the Father will send in my name, will teach you all things and will remind you of everything I have said to you.
>
> John 14:26

> But when he, the Spirit of truth, comes, he will guide you into all truth. He will not speak on his own; he will speak only what he hears, and he will tell you what is yet to come. He will bring glory to me by taking from what is mine and making it known to you.
>
> John 16:13–14

The Spirit illuminates the words of the Bible at times. He also uses words of other individuals in our lives as they speak to us. Their seemingly ordinary words are given the weight of revelation through the Spirit's empowerment. Discernment is another way that the Holy Spirit works within us. We are given insight into the truthfulness of actions, or into consequences stemming from decisions, or even guidance in specific decision-making situations. All of this the Spirit does as an inward presence and strength.

Another action of the Spirit is the giving of spiritual gifts to each believer, some of which have specific application to making good decisions. Spiritual gifts are supernatural gifts, different from personal talents or acquired skills, which are given to believers because they are in Christ Jesus and members of his body. Although the New Testament speaks of the gifts in several different places, perhaps the most direct reference is found in 1 Corinthians 12.

> Now to each one the manifestation of the Spirit is given for the common good. To one there is given through the Spirit the message of wisdom, to another the message of knowledge by means of the same Spirit, to another faith by the same Spirit, to another gifts of healing by that one

Spirit, to another miraculous powers, to another prophecy, to another distinguishing between spirits, to another speaking in different kinds of tongues, and to still another the interpretation of tongues. All these are the work of one and the same Spirit, and he gives them to each one, just as he determines.

1 Corinthians 12:7–11

In this passage some of the gifts of particular note for decision making are wisdom, knowledge, faith, the ability to distinguish between spirits, and even healing. In all of these specific spiritual gifts the Christian is helped by the Holy Spirit in a tangible way to face life's circumstances and challenges. Through the power of the Spirit the Christian is not alone.

The outward presence of the people of God is also a tremendous strength for the Christian. Our English word *church* is derived from the Greek word *kuriakos*, meaning "belonging to the Lord."[9] Every person who belongs to God through a personal relationship with Jesus is a true member of Christ's church and part of a unique family. People in this family are more than just friends or social acquaintances. They are joined together in a truly supernatural bond by the Spirit of God and are "one" with family members from around the world. The church is a universal body of believers. It includes persons from all races, all cultures, and all continents. It is a global group of persons naming Jesus Christ as Lord and participating in the truth of the gospel. With friends all over the world, a Christian is truly never alone.

Once again, the illustration provided by the apostle Paul in 1 Corinthians 12 of the church as "the body of Christ" reminds us that we are interconnected with others in Jesus and that each of us has a function important to the whole.

The body is a unit, though it is made up of many parts; and though all its parts are many, they form one body. So it is with Christ. For we were all baptized by one Spirit into one body—whether Jews or Greeks, slave or free. . . . If one part suffers, every part suffers with it; if one part is honored, every part rejoices with it. Now you are the body of Christ, and each one of you is a part of it.

1 Corinthians 12:12–13a; 26–27

This body image is a particularly vivid way to remind Christian people that they are never really alone. The Christian life is a life of community in the best sense. We are attached to and strengthened by brothers and sisters in Christ who share in our lives just as we share in theirs. According to Paul, members of the body are to bear one another's burdens (Gal. 6:2). This is easy for us since we have an intimacy and a level of understanding for one another that goes beyond the other casual relationships experienced in the neighborhood or workplace. The outward presence of the people of God is an important support for Christians, one that we can draw upon in the worst of personal tragedies.

Pastors and teachers can do a couple of things to ensure that their church family receives the benefits of Christian support. For one, teach those under your care to specifically request spiritual support when they are being admitted to the hospital. With the distractions of the moment, patients and families can easily forget this important part of their support system. There were many times during my pastorates when my congregation members were in medical crisis and didn't even think to phone me or request that I, as their pastor, come to the hospital. Now that I'm a chaplain, I see the suggestion of the notification of a family's minister or priest as one of my first priorities when I am called to support a family.

Second, train hospital visitors or care teams to provide spiritual support if the pastor is unavailable for some reason. Crisis knows no timetable. A pastor can be out of town attending a conference, or be on vacation, or be unavailable because of family reasons when a significant crisis occurs. It is so important in times of pastoral absence to have other spiritual leaders in the congregation who can respond to emergencies and be trained in what to expect at a medical center. This is part of "equipping the saints" and another area of Christian education to be added to all the other important areas of biblical maturity and leadership that are often the focus of attention for pastors and Bible study leaders. A variety of resources and programs are available for training hospital care teams and spiritual advocates. Pastoral leaders would do well to make this a priority in their planning process.

In Summary

In this chapter we have briefly looked at five Christian distinctives that characterize and undergird our unique approach to medical decision making. When facing ethical dilemmas or difficult care decisions, Christians will utilize all of them in one way or another in the personal choices they make. These beliefs and theological commitments stand as a foundation in the lives of Christians who face a mostly secular and rationalistic approach to medicine and care when they interact with medical professionals in our hospitals or care centers. All who call themselves Christians embrace beliefs such as the ones above and draw strength from them during times of crisis. They can all be tremendous resources for the pastoral leader to remember and use as he or she supports friends and families in emergency medical situations.

Notes

1. H. Tristram Engelhardt Jr., *The Foundations of Christian Bioethics* (Lisse, The Netherlands: Swets & Zeitlinger, 2000), 171.

2. St. Isaac the Syrian, *The Ascetical Homilies of Saint Isaac the Syrian,* trans. Holy Transfiguration Monastery (Boston: Holy Transfiguration Monastery, 1984), 227.

3. Millard J. Erickson, *Christian Theology* (Grand Rapids: Baker Books, 1983), 440.

4. James Houston, *The Heart's Desire* (Colorado Springs: NavPress, 1996), 221–22.

5. Engelhardt, *Foundations of Christian Bioethics*, 316–17.

6. Ibid., 317.

7. Ibid., 318.

8. Ibid., 322.

9. Erickson, *Christian Theology,* 1030.

9

Ethical Issues in Death and Dying

I met Tony's family one morning in the surgery waiting room. A local pastor friend caught my eye as I was walking past the waiting room doorway. I went in to say hello to him, and he introduced me to Tony's wife, Karen, who attended his congregation and who was awaiting news about her husband's surgery. She was a mother of three children and in her mid-forties. Karen looked drawn and tired. She was obviously very upset and worried. Karen explained that exploratory surgery was in progress and that they were expecting the worst. Prior to surgery the doctor had told them that several tumors were located around the colon and perhaps the pancreas too. Karen didn't know what this might mean for the future, but in the best case it certainly would entail many more doctor visits and complicate an already busy family schedule. Most of all she was worried about losing the man she loved. After a few words of support and a promise to pray for Tony, I left them to continue my hospital rounds.

A couple of hours later I decided to cruise through the surgery waiting room to check in with Karen to see how things were going. The pastor was standing in the hallway outside the waiting room doorway with five or six other family members when I came into view. He immediately took my arm and walked with me down the hall, away from the group for a private conversation. With an emotion-charged voice he related that the surgeon had informed them that Tony's cancer was so extensive that all he could do was close him back up again and abort any attempt to remove it. This father of three in the prime of his life would soon be told that he had inoperable cancer. According to the surgeon, Tony had but weeks to live. Karen had been so upset when she heard the news that a sister had already taken her home. Her worst fears had been realized.

In the next weeks, as Tony and Karen face terminal illness and Tony's eventual death, their lives will be turned upside down. They had planned for many years to raise their children, see them grow into adulthood, pick life vocations, and get married and start their own families, and then spoil the grandchildren during their retirement while living in a cabin on lake property in the country. This was the expected life pattern they had seen modeled by older family and friends, and it was, in a sense, their American dream. Now that dream was shattered, and a whole host of other losses would soon become apparent to them as well. Death seems so distant in our lives when we're trying to make a living, raise our children, and grow in our career paths. But death can quickly upset our applecart and scatter our dreams and life plans in chaos. In actuality our lives are fragile, and we live every moment within a heartbeat of death. We know down deep that death is a part of life and that we will all die, but we resist thinking about it, and we seem to deny that it will happen to us. Unfortunately, our inability to face death and the dying process is a primary factor clouding objective health-care decision making and leading to ethical dilemmas.

This chapter will look at three areas of ethical concern that are a part of nearly every dying process. The first concerns our human desire for self-determination. Persons seeking physician-assisted suicide often do so because they want control of the dying process. Second, advance care planning and the issues that surround advance directives will be investigated. Third, the impact of personal loss and the resulting anticipatory grief often surprise the family and friends of someone in the process of dying. We will examine possible issues and dynamics associated with grief and its effects upon health-care decision making.

Self-Determination

James was a gruff old fellow with a heart of gold, who came to our hospice program with a diagnosis of lung cancer. Though he had not been a religious person throughout his life, he was willing to allow me to make a few visits and give spirituality one more chance in his life. Our first meeting spawned a wonderful relationship, and I became a regular visitor over the next several months. James and I talked real life issues together, and he pulled no punches. He was the son of an abusive father whom he hated, and so he had run away from home when he was thirteen to make his own way in the world. Through the years he joined the armed forces, did odd jobs, got married, had a family, raised respectable children, and ended up being employed as a highway construction worker. In the years of his life he survived several close brushes with death, and they had prompted within him an interest in spiritual things. He always had the feeling that Someone was watching over him. As a chaplain I was always seeking to help James clarify his belief system and so pushed the conversation to explore his concept of God, belief in the afterlife, and his perception of God's presence through his week-by-week battle with cancer. We enjoyed some wonderful moments in deep conversation together for upward of five months. Then one morning I received a phone call telling me that James had gone into the bedroom with a gun and shot himself in the head! The news stunned me. I was shocked and wondered what I had missed in our times together that would have given a clue to his intentions. When I saw his wife later that same day, she expressed her own disbelief and confusion at what had transpired. He had gotten up that morning, followed his normal routine, and spoken to her as if it were a typical day, and then she heard the gunshot a few moments later. She was horrified at the scene she found in the bedroom. As we sat around the living room talking, not one of the family members said that they had any idea that James would take his own life. There was not a sign given to us that would have pointed to his considering the suicide option. He surprised everyone with an action that seemed incongruent with his everyday conversation and with what we thought to be his personal goals for the future. On the other hand, the family knew that he had kept a gun near his bedside for many years. He was also a no-nonsense type of person and one who had faced life his own way since he was a child. Furthermore, his cancer was beginning to take a toll on his independence and also causing more pain. Putting all these facts together provided some rationale for James's actions, but not all of it. The family, unfortunately, will bear the devastation of James's final solution the rest of their lives.

The fact that James chose to end his life by his own hand is not unusual for someone with a terminal illness. To think about suicide is very common when the future is darkened by an uncertain progression of a terrible illness, with all the pain and suffering that accompanies it. In truth most people in these circumstances at least consider the option. As adult human beings, we are used to planning our lives, taking responsibility for our own futures, and having the control to go where we want to go and do what we want to do. The intrusion of a sickness that might sap our strength, limit our independence, and impose restrictions on our activities fills us with dread and in many persons raises contemplation of the ultimate act of independence and self-determination. There is a certain safety in being able to control when and how death comes. With suicide also comes control over loss of financial resources and over the impact that the cost of a lengthy illness will have on our families.

I have two adult female friends who are both single, both live adventurous lives as mountaineers, and both recently stated that they don't want to die in a hospital under any circumstances. We were tent camping and sitting around the picnic table when the subject of how we wanted to die came up in the conversation. Deborah related that she doesn't have any health insurance and has worked very hard throughout her life to have a home and a small savings account. She emphatically told us, "I don't want to go to the hospital if I get sick. I'm sixty-three years old, and I've already got a friend all picked out who has promised to take me into the forest and leave me when I'm chronically ill. I won't go into the hospital. I think it's robbery for them to take all that I've worked for throughout my life. I would rather die peacefully at a younger age in the forest alone." Pat, on the other hand, has health insurance, a good job teaching at a community college, and should have no worries financially. But she added to the conversation by saying, "I don't want all those tubes in me that the hospital insists on inserting. I would never want to be on life support. I plan on dying in the mountains. I'll go there when it's my time." Though the odds are that Deborah and Pat will find themselves in the hospital someday, intubated against their best-laid plans because of some bodily infection or perhaps a cardiac/respiratory arrest, the personal self-determination and control that they desire over their last days is clearly important to them.

Similarly, those persons who seek physician-assisted suicide or euthanasia often do so because they desire to be in control of their own fate. Though a common argument for physician-assisted suicide is based upon inordinate and intolerable pain and suffering, many of the individuals who truly ask for physician assistance in ending their life do so because of a strong belief in this self-determination ideal, which permeates our society and is, in fact, accepted by the majority of people in the United States. Christian bioethicist Tristram Engelhardt points to this problem when he writes: "If a society values individual choice and self-determination regarding ways of life, it should presumptively value individual choice and self-determination regarding death. In a liberal cosmopolitan culture that celebrates autonomy, life or death outside of personal control will be experienced as personally demeaning, alienating, and undignified."[1] Christian people will find themselves struggling ethically with these issues as they interact with friends and neighbors who choose to follow this and other societal norms and are uninformed of biblical cautions against self-centeredness or self-rule.

In another area of ethical difficulty associated with the subject of suicide, I have met several Christian people who as patients had a personal struggle with limiting treatment that was futile because of a personal commitment against suicide. For instance, one very devout lady had an awful bone cancer that had metastasized throughout her body. When she was eventually unable to eat, she questioned whether she should have a feeding tube inserted to provide nutrition. The hospice social worker and I had been counseling her to accept her coming death and to, with courage, "let go" and let her faith be her strength. In exploring her theological beliefs, I finally discovered that she felt that to "not do everything" was the same thing as deciding upon suicide. To her, to decline the feeding tube was the same thing as willfully seeking an end to her life. Some people have called decisions to withhold a life-sustaining measure "passive euthanasia." It took some processing of feelings and a revised theological outlook for her to trust God, to stop treatment, and to "let nature take its course" in acceptance of God's will. We had to convince her that she was not committing suicide by deciding to forgo the tube feedings. There is no dishonor in accepting death as a normal part of life. In fact, to do so brings dignity to the human struggle and glorifies God in the process. In speaking of a Christian ethical approach to this issue of causation of death Engelhardt again writes:

> Christians may stop treatment and "let nature take its course" in humble acceptance of God's will. As such, they do not cause death. This interpretation of causation highlights particular duties and discloses particular spiritual dangers. It recognizes a distinction between withholdings or withdrawings that are passive homicide or passive euthanasia, versus withholdings and withdrawings that amount to letting God's will be

done. Even outside of traditional Christianity, one can distinguish between omissions not undertaken in order to bring an early death and those that are intentionally focused on achieving an earlier demise. The second are properly instances of passive euthanasia. . . . The traditional Christian approach . . . focuses primarily (albeit not exclusively) on intention and the avoidance of proximate causal involvement in the death of a human.[2]

Roman Catholic theologians have based their decisions in such cases upon the ethical principle of "double effect." A treatment with potential negative outcome can be utilized if the *intent* of the treatment is to help the patient. For instance, high doses of morphine may be given to relieve pain, even with the knowledge that at some point the high dose may also repress the breathing of the patient and cause death. There are two "effects" from the administration of the painkiller, but the intended effect was to relieve the patient's pain. Engelhardt, an Eastern Orthodox Christian, realizes the ambiguity in such decisions and still recognizes the importance of seeking God's guidance and grace in decision making circumstances. Christians must not intend to kill by omission but instead to help the patient, out of a motivation of love and concern. He warns of the "spiritual danger of being proximately involved in taking the life of another, even if this be fully involuntary."[3] Again, *intent* is where the key element lies. In the ethics of decision making, understanding the intent of a decision supersedes individual acts. "An act can be wrong even if it achieves good results, and an act can be right even if some of its effects are evil."[4]

Ethical dilemmas in decision making that center on the theme of suicide are very common in the minds of patients who have a terminal illness and are facing eventual death. As we have seen, they are also common in treatment decisions that involve withholding or withdrawing life-support measures or terminal sedation. Ambiguity is part of the problem.

Advance Care Planning

In many instances people are brought to the hospital unconscious and in need of a variety of treatment measures before they are able to give consent. Emergency department physicians follow standards of care that exist for each diagnostic need until they are able to talk with family members or another representative who can speak legally to the specific care wishes of the patient. If the patient is elderly, has a terminal illness or other chronic health problem, or for some reason would decline aspects of standard medical treatment (e.g., a Jehovah's Witness, who would not want blood transfusions), ethical dilemmas often become apparent, since treatment has been started and suddenly a change in treatment must be instituted to follow the wishes of family members or the patient. As we have noted, treatment interventions once instituted are often not easily rescinded. For instance, once a blood transfusion has been started, it is impossible to extract the blood from the Jehovah's Witness. Other dilemmas occur when family members disagree about what the patient might want done or when open conflict between family members clouds the care picture. The complications of these situations can be exponentially reduced if the patient has given thought to advance care planning. This refers to the documenting of specific personal wishes regarding heroic treatment measures for end of life, as well as the appointing of a surrogate decision maker, that is, someone who is very aware of the patient's wishes in a variety of life-threatening health-care scenarios and can legally speak for the patient. Documents that specify patient wishes are called *advance directives.* There are several types of advance directives that are important to know about and on which we will now focus.

Durable Power of Attorney for Health Care

This document is a signed, witnessed, and notarized legal recognition of someone designated by the patient to speak, act, and write for them in the event they are unable to do so themselves. A durable power of attorney for health care is not the same as a *financial* durable power of attorney. Durable power of attorney for *health care* is honored in health-care institutions by physicians and other medical caregivers. It does not require an attorney to draft, and various formats that require only two witnesses and perhaps a notary public are readily found and distributed by hospitals. Its function is to designate a surrogate *decision maker* and has nothing to do with financial responsibility. Often a spouse, a son or daughter, or a parent is chosen by the patient for this role. This person then becomes *the* decision maker on behalf of the patient in all health-care decisions, once again, *only if* the patient cannot make the decisions for himself or herself. Needless to say, this is an awesome responsibility to shoulder and a position requiring great trust. Having someone with your durable power, however, is the best guarantee that your wishes will be followed. It also helps one avoid a myriad of possible misunderstandings or even open conflict. I recommend that every adult have a durable power of attorney for health care. If you don't have one, misunderstandings can easily occur. The Jones family, for instance, had to face a situation that turned into a nightmare, made more difficult for them all because there was no designated durable power of attorney for health care.

Leonard Jones entered the hospital with a lung infection that should have been easily remedied after a round of antibiotics. He was a non-smoker and an otherwise healthy sixty-two-year-old. But for some unknown reason the infection continued to have a hold on him, and within a couple of days he was transferred to the ICU, intubated, and placed on a breathing machine in hopes of taking the pressure off his lungs and letting them heal. But even with an additional round of antibiotics, things went from bad to worse. His lungs did not respond. After an extended stay in ICU, Leonard was diagnosed with adult respiratory distress syndrome. His lungs became unable to inflate by themselves and he was dependent upon the ventilator. His doctors told the family that this was a nonsurvivable condition. Because of the suddenness of the downturn and Leonard's previous vitality, they took this news very hard. The Jones family gathered at the hospital and began a vigil of support for Leonard. Earlier, and before Leonard slipped into unconsciousness, he had told the doctor that he didn't want to be on a breathing machine if his prognosis was poor. But with him now unconscious, his family was left struggling with his care decisions. Leonard's elderly mother found herself supporting the physician's recommendation to withdraw the life support and let Leonard go, as difficult as it would be for her to lose her son. But Leonard's daughter approached her father's care from a divergent viewpoint.

Lisa was a highly religious person who loved life and valued spiritual reflection when it came to making life decisions. To see her father helpless on the breathing machine, unable to move his body, and dependent upon those taking care of him raised in her a daughter's sense of protection. The prospect of his death was more than she could take. It was like losing part of herself.[5] Something seemed wrong to her about just turning off the machine and in a sense "putting her father to death." In fact, she would not allow it. She told the doctor that this could not be done, and in the face of Leonard's mother and every other close family member, she dissented at the care conference. The physician and family found themselves at an impasse. Throughout the next couple of days Lisa counseled with her spiritual leaders and held fast to her disagreement at withdrawing life support. The rest of the family was speechless at the drama being played out and were unwilling to get involved, rendered powerless by their own uncertainty about the medical diagnosis and what was the right thing to do. The physician attempted to bring in other colleagues to lend support to his diagnosis, as well as the hospital chaplain and social worker to support and educate the family. After several days, inordinate medical costs, and great heartache on all sides, Leonard's end finally came. But how much better it would have been if Leonard had been able to designate one person to speak on his behalf, and to relieve his daughter and the rest of the family of the responsibility of making a hard decision.

Designating someone to have your durable power of attorney for health care is an important decision. But the choice alone is not the end of the matter, for then you must have a long conversation with your new representative on a variety of crucial topics. Physician Bruce Bartlow suggests you share honestly your life goals, hopes, fears, quality of life before and after the illness, burdens of therapy proposed (for instance, CPR), and benefits of therapy acceptable (e.g., survival versus function).[6] The latest suggestions for completing advance planning documents strongly recommend that "thresholds" of medical interventions be stipulated in the advance directive as a means of determining acceptable levels of treatment. In whatever form you choose to relay your wishes, your representative must take good notes and be as fully informed as possible concerning your desires in these most important life issues. Recent research has focused on the decision-making congruency of the patient and the "surrogate" decision maker, often finding that the surrogate's personal concerns interfere with the following of explicit patient wishes in a surprising number of cases.[7] The more you can assure your representative of your true wishes, the more secure that person will be in advocating on your behalf. This brings us to a second type of advance directive form.

Five Wishes

"Five Wishes" is a comprehensive *living will* form that seeks to incorporate personal, emotional, and spiritual desires—as well as medical ones—concerning end-of-life care into five specific "wishes" of the patient. Five Wishes originated through the efforts of a special man. "For 12 years, a man named Jim Towey worked closely with Mother Teresa, and, for one year, he lived in a hospice she ran in Washington, D.C. Inspired by this first-hand experience, Mr. Towey sought a way for patients and their families to plan ahead and to cope with serious illness. The result is Five Wishes and the response to it has been overwhelming. . . . Newspapers have called Five Wishes the first 'living will with a heart.' "[8] A durable power of attorney for health care is included in the Five Wishes format. Five Wishes also gives people the opportunity to speak to the kind of medical treatment they want or don't want, pain management issues, personal spiritual wishes at time of death, and even funeral arrangements. The format can be viewed on the following website: www.agingwithdignity.org. I find it to be an excellent tool for end-of-life planning, and I highly recommend its use.

Comfort One (At Home Do Not Resuscitate)

A third advance care planning tool is a do-not-resuscitate (DNR) directive for terminal patients who live outside the hospital. It is available in most states and is sometimes called "Comfort One." This legal directive allows terminally ill patients to wear a bracelet or have a "notice" in their home that declares they do not want CPR or heroic life-sustaining measures should they have a cardiac or respiratory arrest. When EMTs or ambulance crews arrive on the scene and see the Comfort One designation, they provide comfort measures and treat the patient medically, but without CPR or other heroic interventions. This advance directive came about because too many people with terrible cancers or other terminal health conditions were resuscitated against their will and brought to the ER by emergency responders. A Comfort One or similar home-based DNR order allows a suffering patient to die with dignity and at home, according to his or her wishes.

Advance care planning is a particularly important area of education for all pastors and other spiritual leaders who have oversight of congregations and families. Upon admission to hospitals and medical centers, all adult patients (of any age) are now being asked if they have an advance directive/living will, or if not, whether they have thought about advance care planning. It is an important teaching responsibility to address this aspect of medical care in our churches and education groups in order to make our flocks aware of the medical issues they may face and to apply discipleship to this crucial area of life. I urge you to take the initiative and learn more about what you can do as a pastor or priest to ensure that those under your care can be assured that they will have their faith beliefs, traditions, and spiritual needs addressed by the health-care institution they frequent. The time will come when they and you will be glad you did.

Personal Loss and Grief

It should not surprise us that people are uncomfortable with death. And that includes you and me. The death of significant others is painful to us. And unfortunately, many decision-making choices are influenced by our own personal issues and lack of self-awareness about how we feel about death and dying. A third area often spawning ethical dilemmas has to do with the personal loss and grief issues of family and friends. A common experience is illustrated by what happened with Jane when she found out she had terminal cancer.

Jane was a single lady in her mid-fifties when she started experiencing a tightness around her waist and abdomen. A visit to her personal doctor culminated in the scheduling of lab tests, an MRI scan, and eventually the diagnosis of liver cancer. Jane had only a few months to live. She wondered how to proceed. It was a devastating blow to receive such horrible news. She called her good friend Marg and told her about the diagnosis. Marg came right over and sat with Jane as they cried together. It felt good to have someone to talk to. Jane was uncertain how much to tell other friends, because she was worried they might treat her differently, but when she went to church that weekend she asked for prayer in her small group circle. She had many of her church friends come up to her that day and give their sympathies. Many said they would continue to pray for her. In the following weeks, Jane ran into several of the church friends at the mall and around town. She noticed that they always asked about her illness, how she was coping, and other questions surrounding doctor visits or her pain level, but they seemed quick to end the conversation after she replied to a few of the questions and then they hurried on giving a typical excuse about another commitment. As the weeks went by, many of her church friends just lowered their heads when she walked past them, or seemed involved in other conversations. Jane was beginning to feel like she had the plague and that they were avoiding her. Marg, on the other hand, visited her several times a week at home, and they had good conversations. At the two-month anniversary of Jane's diagnosis she was beginning to appear jaundiced, and other physical symptoms were escalating. Jane could see her end coming. When she tried to talk with Marg about death and dying, Marg very uncharacteristically chided her about being negative concerning her chances of survival. Jane was told to "have faith and maintain a positive approach, because attitude and personal confidence influences survival chances and quality of life." Jane was disappointed in Marg's unwillingness to listen to her. Of course she knew that a positive attitude was helpful in fighting her disease, but she was dying! She needed someone to listen to her talk about her fears, her doubts, and the losses she was beginning to experience as strength waned and her world caved in upon her. Over the weeks of her illness Jane found herself more and more isolated from friends and activities. They just didn't mean as much to her as they did previously. She read the Bible and slept a lot. Her greatest desire was to truly have a friend to walk with her through this final stage of her life.

Jane's experience is unfortunately typical of the type of stigma faced by persons with a terminal illness. Support systems break down, good friends may avoid contact, and the result is a lonelier and more desperate journey for the one person everyone would like to help the most. If we as spiritual leaders, counselors, and elders can become aware of this very human tendency toward avoidance and stigma, perhaps we can bring awareness to those we disciple about fear of death, the dynamics of grief and loss, and how to support a person with a terminal illness. Then perhaps we can be of greater support for people like Jane when we are called upon to be a true friend and spiritual advocate.

Anticipatory Grief

The type of grieving that occurs before a person dies is called *anticipatory grief*. When we find out that we have a friend or family member who is terminal, anticipatory grieving is what we do. It concerns all the feelings and the emotions that we have as we realize that someone very important in our lives will soon be gone. In our minds we begin to review the history of our relationship with the individual—both the positive and the negative history. Sometimes guilt issues arise as we think about times when we were "not at our best" in the relationship. And there can be an experience of *denial* that suddenly takes hold of us as the thought of losing this valuable person becomes too much to bear. It is too overwhelming to consider how *our* lives will change once this person is gone. If we've had other recent losses, such as other deaths, a divorce, a job failure, family alienation, relocation, a physical illness, or a crisis, or for some reason feel insecure in our present lives, then, human dynamics being what they are, we actually seek to maintain a sense of stability and fight change and deny another potential loss, that is, the terminally ill friend we *can't* bear to lose.

Many of the ethical dilemmas I have observed in dealing with families in ER or ICU settings as they face the possible death of someone they love center on attempts to go beyond standards of care and what would be considered medically appropriate treatment, because of the personal inability to let go and accept the fact that the patient will die. The families insist on trying another intervention or other protocols even when the interventions are medically futile. The ER or ICU staff then find themselves ethically challenged as they attempt to meet the requests of grieving families. Physicians are very aware of the possibility of litigation should they be perceived by the family as not "doing all that can be done," so they acquiesce to perceived family demands. This, in effect, turns into a situation where the family is *overmanaging* the patient's medical care, simply because of denial and personal issues of a loss/grief nature.

Grief therapist William Worden observed a situation such as this where it was obvious that mixed motives were subtly affecting medical decision making. He writes:

> I observed one woman whose husband was a patient in the hospital's private service. She wanted to keep her husband alive and went to the most extreme means, extreme even to the most conservative of medical opinion. On the surface it looked to the nurses and other people caring for the patient like she cared so much for her husband that she wanted to keep him alive against all odds. But you only had to scratch the surface slightly to see that this woman had an extremely ambivalent relationship with her husband and she was expressing her ambivalence through this oversolicitation.[9]

This woman probably felt some guilt because of the less-than-satisfying relationship with her husband. In many instances, loving family members also oversolicit medical care. Worden emphasizes that "denying the facts of the loss can vary in degree from a sight distortion to a full-blown delusion."[10] In some cases people have, after the death of a loved one, been unable to say good-bye to the body and have kept the deceased in the house for days without notifying anyone about the death! Other similarly bizarre death reactions have been well documented.

Another dynamic of anticipatory grief has to do with an increase in personal death awareness, that is, awareness of our own death. When we are around someone fighting death's battle, we are confronted with our own humanness and the fact that we too will die at some time in the future. The fear of facing our own mortality is one of the major causes of the uncomfortable feelings we have in conversing with someone with a terminal illness. This fear can subtly affect how we act or respond to the ill person, usually manifested in an avoidance of them or an inability to talk with them about certain difficult topics—the dying process, death, spirituality, or loss in general. As an advocate, you must be able to listen and to accept what you hear.

Grief and the Challenge to Personal Life Perceptions

A second significant grief reaction experienced by family or friends of a terminally ill patient has to do with the challenge that dying and death pose to perceptions of life and the way things go in the world. Death raises questions in us regarding the meaning of life, the goodness of the universe, spiritual beliefs, and fundamental values. Questions such as: Why did this happen? Why this person? Why now? Where is God in this? Why is life unfair? Why does evil exist? Is what I previously believed instead false? Death is, after all, a violation of our core belief that we have a right to life and is an assault on the high value we place upon life. Death is antithetical to what we hear in secular television commercials and read in magazines about "taking life by the horns" and living the Great American Dream. We have been taught in our culture to be responsible for our lives, as well as the lives of our children and others that we love, and to believe we have personal control in matters of career success and future endeavors. When death suddenly bursts into our lives, the control we thought we had is no more. Instead we find ourselves confused, vulnerable, our beliefs held in question, our orderly world shattered, our predicted future instead turned upside down.

Anger, anxiety, guilt, self-blame, fear, and victimization are only a few of the reactions stemming from such a challenge to our normal life expectations. In supporting the terminally ill, these personal issues once again cause us problems. The supportive relationship becomes suddenly complicated, and authentic interaction becomes overlaid with meanings and concerns that can only impair the supportive atmosphere. In medical decision-making situations, anger, blame, and the search for a "reason why" can be shifted to medical personnel and staff responsible for caring for the patient, and great misunderstandings (creating ethical issues) can often result. A theological foundation and medical awareness that provide a solid ground for supporting people in the face of adversity and the evil of suffering and death does much to empower the advocate, family member, or friend as they seek to journey with one who is terminally ill. Awareness is the key. Teach your church family about the dynamics of grief and loss.

In summary, we have examined three areas of ethical concern that surround death and dying: self-determination and suicide, advance care planning and advance directives, and the personal loss and grief issues of those supporting a dying patient. All three have an effect upon advocacy and decision-making choices, with many potential ethical dilemmas stemming from the issues raised in these areas.

Notes

1. H. Tristram Engelhardt Jr., *The Foundations of Christian Bioethics* (Lisse, The Netherlands: Swets & Zeitlinger, 2000), 312.

2. Ibid., 320.

3. Ibid., 321.

4. The President's Council on Bioethics, *Taking Care: Ethical Caregiving in Our Aging Society* (Washington, DC: President's Council on Bioethics, September 2005), 142.

5. Samira K. Beckwith, "When Families Disagree: Family Conflict and Decisions," in *Ethical Dilemmas at the End of Life*, ed. Kenneth J. Doka, Bruce Jennings, and Charles A. Corr (Washington, DC: Hospice Foundation of America, 2005), 152.

6. Bruce G. Bartlow, *Medical Care of the Soul: A Practical and Healing Guide to End-of-Life Issues for Families, Patients, and Healthcare Providers* (Boulder, CO: Johnson Printing, 2000), 28.

7. The reader is referred to research of Respecting Choices, Gundersen Lutheran Medical Foundation, 1836 South Ave., La Crosse, WI, 54601. See their Web page: www.gundluth.org/eolprograms.

8. "Aging with Dignity, Five Wishes", (Tallahassee, FL: Aging with Dignity, 2001). See their website: www.agingwithdignity.org.

9. J. William Worden, *Grief Counseling & Grief Therapy: A Handbook for the Mental Health Practitioner* (New York: Springer, 1991), 110.

10. Ibid., 11.

10

Spiritual Interventions by the Advocate

It is an awesome responsibility to be placed in the position of spiritual advocate by someone you love and care for. In my more than twenty years of ministry, I have never felt adequate for the task. There is a certain feeling of incompetence that I always feel when called to be with someone in a moment of crisis. Often the phone call comes suddenly from a special "friend in the faith," someone with whom I have had deep and meaningful conversations about my trust in God and from whom I have received support and strength in *my* Christian walk. When I hear the frantic report that a family member was just taken in an ambulance, first my heart rate increases, my breathing becomes faster, and an aroused feeling of urgency envelops my every move as I search for what I might need to get myself to the hospital quickly. All the while a sense of compassion for my good friend floods my body, and a hope for the best outcome underlies my search for a coat and car keys. Once in the car, it dawns on me that this experience greatly impacts my *own* life, despite what is happening to my friend and his family member. I reflect on the fact that I am being called to be a part of a potential life-and-death drama that is not just the plot of a movie I am watching or something that I am reading in a novel. This is real life, with real consequences, real feelings, and real fear. At this point I might start wondering what personal resources I have to bring to this situation. I might even question why I was the one that was called. Wouldn't someone else be better at this? Isn't there someone else who is more qualified or more spiritually ready for what is to come? Yet I keep on driving and offer a prayer asking God to guide me and give me wisdom when I finally meet my friend. It is a humbling and scary position to be in when you are called to be an advocate in such circumstances.

And yet chances are *you* will have this experience someday. It is best to be equipped to meet the challenge and as ready as possible to be a spiritual advocate when God puts you in that position. That is what this book has been about. And so the final part of our preparation concerns the variety of interventions that an advocate must become aware of and able to draw upon in a crisis or decision-making situation. Although there are many interventions besides the following, in my experience these are the most important.

Presence

As you enter a crisis situation, what you say is not nearly as important as "being there" and accompanying the friend or parishioner in the journey they are having to make. For them, it is a gift that you are just able to be present. They are walking an uncertain and unfamiliar pathway, in an often impersonal and foreign medical world of technology, instruments, masks, and white coats. They are being separated from the one they love during medical procedures and deeply feel the distance and inability to have personal control as frightening limitations. To have a friend at their side is a very real and significant gift. It is what is needed most.

Unfortunately, the importance of presence and just "being there" for someone in a crisis is a ministry that pastors and religious leaders need to evaluate and revisit in their own personal ministry practice. In my years of hospital chaplaincy I have sat with many worried families and provided presence when their own priest or pastor was for some reason unavailable or too busy to spend time with them. It was very common to have religious leaders meet the family of a patient in the ICU waiting room for a quick prayer, or to offer the Eucharist, only to have them leave shortly thereafter feeling they had done all they could do as a professional minister. To you priests, pastors, elders, and deacons I would submit that *little else* in your daily schedule has true priority over *being there* for a frightened family member as he or she waits for the outcome of a critical medical intervention in the life of a loved one! It is your *presence* with family members during such tense moments that they will remember the rest of their lives. The "being there" is what solidifies Christian friendships and brings deeper relationships in the body of Christ. It is also the best thing we do as a representative of God.

When we are requested by someone to take up the role of spiritual friend and advocate, we become a representative of God in their lives. The apostle Paul speaks of this ministry when he writes to the Corinthians:

> Praise be to the God and Father of our Lord Jesus Christ, the Father of compassion and the God of all comfort, who comforts us in all our troubles, so that we can comfort those in any trouble with the comfort we ourselves have received from God.
>
> 2 Corinthians 1:3–4

> We are therefore Christ's ambassadors, as though God were making his appeal through us.
>
> 2 Corinthians 5:20a

As we sit with our friends in that crucial time of waiting that is so much a part of the hospital experience, we represent Christ as his ambassador to them. Our presence is a sign that God is with them and that he cares and knows what is happening to them. Our continual presence with them is a reminder that God is faithful and that he will not leave them or abandon them. William Arnold writes the following regarding faithfulness and the theological significance it holds for pastoral care:

> Models for the exercise of faithfulness are to be found throughout Scripture. God's faithfulness to Israel, the keeping of the covenant, Hosea's faithfulness to Gomer, the frequent references to marriage as paradigmatic to God's faithfulness, the death and resurrection of Jesus—all characterize for us the content of faithfulness. A demanding principle, it distinctively illustrates what it means to care in a pastoral manner.[1]

Presence is defined by faithfulness. To be faithful to someone is to stay with them throughout the time they are in crisis. It is a sign of God's grace and love when we commit to being available and present and willing to give attention to one of his beloved children. In this there is no expectation of return. There is no expectation of response. Presence can be given in silence, without conversation. Presence can be expressed merely in an occasional touch of a hand, or a hug, or just in sitting next to one another for hours without any other interaction. The caring happens without dependence upon external expressions.

Presence also offers freedom to the friend who asked us to be there. Sometimes aloneness is important. Just because we are present doesn't mean we need never leave someone's side. Our friend may be grateful to us but may also need times of privacy and solitude. I make it a practice to leave the room often during such times. Experiment with length of times during which you intentionally leave your friend alone. Offer to go get a drink or some food. Take a walk down the hall or to the hospital chapel for prayer. Be ever vigilant to subtle signs where they say "no" to your caring presence. When we offer something that we *think* expresses care, recognize that the time may not be right.

Since we are merely human beings, remember that our perceptions of someone else's need may be incorrect. We cannot know everything our friend is thinking or experiencing. When a "no" is given, accept it gracefully and without personal judgment. In all of your time together, be present but unobtrusive. Seek to discern what they need from you and provide support as appropriately as possible. Presence is a subtle support. It is the most important and fundamental support we can give as spiritual advocates.

Listening

Spiritual leaders are used to telling people what to do. Most often those mature in Christ have grown into the role of pastor/teacher and have taught a variety of group Bible studies or Christian education classes, or have otherwise "discipled" new Christians in the faith. If ministering in the role of parish pastor, then a whole range of preaching, teaching, and exhorting functions have been internalized by the spiritual leader, making him/her a veritable fountain of information and doctrinal truth. If, as an advocate, a leader brings these pastoral instincts into the hospital, then the default course of action is for them to take over and tell people what to do. But this is exactly what you cannot do as an advocate. As an advocate your role is to listen and clarify and accept—but not *to do*. It is a completely unnatural thing for leaders to relearn. But an advocate must learn it.

True listening is a skill that takes time to develop. It is itself a discipline and takes hard work. But there are times in our lives when all we crave is someone to listen to us. I remember being called to the room of a man in his fifties who was recently diagnosed with terminal cancer. As soon as I sat down and made myself comfortable, he began to talk about his life. He told me all about his family and children and the struggles with each child relationship over the years. He related his personal regrets in not providing a better home for them and more financial security. He told me how much he loved his wife and that he had been faithful to her despite several opportunities with other women through the years. And then he talked about his future and disappointment that he would not be able to have the time of retirement that he had worked so hard to achieve. His personal faith came through in line after line of monologue, and he just kept going on. I never said a word for over an hour! This man just needed someone to listen to him. Finally, at the end he said, "Thank you for all your help." I blessed him and left the room, wondering what help I had really offered. What I had done was simply listen, but in the process I had ascribed value to him and acceptance of his journey through life. Listening is a true act of love.

Gary Sweeten in his excellent book *Listening for Heaven's Sake* enumerates several benefits of actively listening to someone. He writes the following about what he calls the Helper and Seeker relationship:

> Seekers develop a deep sense of trust in a Helper when they feel understood and listened to. The Seeker sets the pace and determines the amount and type of information to share. Given this kind of freedom, Seekers are far more likely to share an open, honest and complete picture of their inner thoughts and feelings. Usually Seekers discover thoughts and feelings they were never consciously aware of before. They gain new and deeper insights into themselves and into new options for changing their lives for the better.[2]

To develop such a trusting relationship is a major milestone for the spiritual advocate. In addition, the processing that occurs as people verbalize their thoughts and feelings, getting them out in the open, is a means of self-counsel that helps the person clarify relevant issues and come to resolution of personal conflicts. After talking for awhile, they will often say, "Now I know what I should do." Listening is a key element in facilitating this new self-awareness. So how can you be a better listener?

A primary method for developing the skill of listening is called *active* or *reflective listening*. It is made up of three components, once again summarized by Gary Sweeten:[3]

Identify the *feeling* content that you hear expressed.

Identify the *thought* content that you hear expressed.

Tentatively summarize or paraphrase what you hear in your own words.

Because as human beings we tend to interpret what someone says to us through our own grid of feelings, understandings, or cultural norms, it is very helpful for us to "check out" our understanding of what has been communicated to us. Hence, a tentative summary or paraphrase of what we *think* we heard or perceived about their thoughts or feelings is very important. In other words, since it's impossible for us to read another person's heart or mind, we need to learn to respond in ways that will bring us clarification and allow the communicator to restate the message. Several possible *reflective* responses are:

It sounds like . . .

I'm not sure I'm following you, but . . .

I think I heard you say . . .

Correct me if I'm wrong, but . . .

I wonder if you're feeling . . .

I hear you saying that . . .

Any of the above responses from the listener helps the communicator know that you are trying to understand exactly what is being said to you. And the person also realizes that you are genuinely concerned about them and that you respect their thoughts and ideas on the subject. Being tentative in response is a communication *enabler* that brings to the communicator feelings of "being heard" by a compassionate and empathetic listener.

In short, the skill of listening is one of the most important resources for the advocate when accompanying a friend or parishioner in crisis. It is prompted by respect for the feelings of the one in crisis and is an acknowledgment that no one has *all* the answers or can presume to know *what* is in the heart or mind of another person. Though it might be easy for the advocate to take charge, take control, and prescribe a course of action, such a response must be resisted. The better course is to humbly listen, clarify, and come alongside the one in crisis in a noncoercive and respectful attitude of compassion and love.

Prayer

In responding to crisis situations, I have seen time after time that the person with a heart for God will pray, while others with no faith background will not even *think* about prayer. When faced with the possible loss of someone close to us, we as human beings inevitably feel inadequate and helpless, and it is in those times that seeds of faith sprout and we seek the face of the One who has life in his hands. For such persons with seeds of faith, nothing can substitute for prayer in dire circumstances. It is a much welcomed means of support. On the other hand, for those persons with no concept of God, who have no seed, or for some reason avoid God, prayer is far from their experience and may even upset them if given by a third party, such as a spiritual support advocate. For such persons prayer can be inappropriate or, worse still, a barrier to a supportive relationship. Sometimes their feelings of inadequacy and helplessness are acted out in anger or hostility. Heightened negative emotions can be focused toward the health-care team or even toward the spiritual-care advocate. Thus, spoken prayer in itself cannot be assumed to be a standard intervention for every family or every advocacy situation. This may surprise you, because prayer is so important, but its outward use must be evaluated and appraised in every crisis context. I see the propensity to pray as a test of a person's spiritual maturity and a window into one's inner life. It has provided me with a new understanding of the significance of Romans 10:13: "Everyone who calls on the name of the Lord will be saved." Prayer, and whether it is welcomed or subtly rejected, provides a measuring stick for the discerning spiritual leader who seeks to understand the spiritual heart of someone undergoing crisis.

For the spiritual advocate, however, prayer is usually one of the first actions engaged in when the call comes to respond to crisis. We don't know what we will be facing when we get to the medical center or bedside. Our human limitations and lack of education or crisis intervention skills are suddenly at the forefront of our minds. We realize our need of guidance from God and the wisdom to make right decisions when the full impact of the unfolding events hits us. We don't know what will be required of us or the emotional toll it will inevitably exact. So we pray and pray hard that God will provide us what we need and give us strength and faith and knowledge by his indwelling Holy Spirit. Many prayers calling upon God have been offered in the automobile as the trip is made to meet a family member. God honors prayer stemming from weakness and from a humble and contrite heart.

But when on the scene and surrounded by fearful and emotionally upset family members, what does the advocate pray for? Is prayer for extended life always appropriate? Is it wrong to offer potentially false hope if a fatal event has been sustained by the patient? Do we dare pray against the prognosis of the physicians? What would God truly have us to pray in any given circumstance as an advocate concerned about the spiritual welfare of the ones we are there to represent? The answer to these questions must come from the Spirit and the Word of God to us in each setting. There are no pat answers or formulas for knowing God's will. In our weakness we can hold tightly to the promises of God. For instance, in Romans 8:26–27 Paul encourages us with these words:

> In the same way, the Spirit helps us in our weakness. We do not know what we ought to pray for, but the Spirit himself intercedes for us with groans that words cannot express. And he who searches our hearts knows the mind of the Spirit, because the Spirit intercedes for the saints in accordance with God's will.

The promise is that the Spirit will intercede in each situation for us in accordance with God's will. At least we know this will be happening behind the visible reality confronting us! The prayers we offer out loud must also be prompted by the Spirit and our words given by God's inspiration. This said, there are several insights that I have gained regarding crisis prayer that can be offered for your consideration.

First, prayers for safety and security of the patient meet the patient's immediate needs as well as the needs of the waiting family and friends. Families who know that the patient had serious enough injuries to be brought to the hospital, and know that the medical team is working on their loved one, are very fearful about the pain the patient is experiencing and are concerned about his or her ultimate safety and security. In such situations I often pray a prayer similar to this:

> Our loving God, thank you for your presence in this terrible situation. We ask that you will be with John as he is being helped by the doctors and nurses. Protect him, Father, by your grace and keep him safe as the team works to stabilize his condition and attend to his wounds. Ease his pain. Give him peace. And if he is conscious, O God, surround him with

your strength and be his shield. Give him faith and a trust that comes only from you in times like this. Help him to pray and call upon your name. In Jesus's name we pray, Amen.

This is a prayer for the patient, but those you are praying *with* are also touched by the power of God and in faith know that God will oversee the ultimate safety of their loved one. This is a needed assurance in times when medical procedures force a separation between patient and family, just when family feelings of lack of control are accentuated and all-consuming. They can know that God is there.

Second, prayers for healing are important and necessary (James 5:13–15). In most instances I recommend praying for the bodily healing of someone who has been injured or who is in mortal danger. Jesus's ministry was marked by the healing of diseases and bodily infirmities, and we follow Jesus's example by touching, anointing, and praying for healing. Anyone who has spent time in hospital ministry is aware that God does heal and that sometimes prayer brings health that cannot be explained by science alone. Miracles happen. But God does not always heal. And all human beings will eventually die (or be changed when Christ returns!). In some instances, why not pray for the "full healing" that will take place only when we finally say good-bye to this world and are welcomed by Jesus into heaven? Prayers for healing also provide an occasion for the advocate to educate families and friends about Christian theology and the Christian worldview. As Paul writes in opposition to earthly concerns:

> But our citizenship is in heaven. And we eagerly await a Savior from there, the Lord Jesus Christ.
>
> Philippians 3:20

Finally, a third type of crisis prayer is concerned with reframing negative thoughts a family might have about God. We should all be aware of the fact that sometimes tragedy can bring alienation from God. Some persons have fallen away from belief in God because of a life tragedy. For example, many marginally religious fathers and mothers have faithfully prayed for their children and asked God to protect them. So when tragedy strikes their child and the parents in fear and out of personal guilt (stemming from their own inadequate spiritual commitments) blame God, or experience God as uncaring, there is a real potential that a deeper alienation from God can be the result. Prayer, if welcomed, can act as an intervention to affirm God's presence in the tragedy and remind the parents that God cares for their child and will continue to be with the child throughout the crisis. To know that God not only exists, but very much cares for their child, is something that will provide hope for them in the midst of what is every parent's nightmare. I remember being in the ER with a mother and father who attended church only three or four times a year. Their daughter had been hit by a car and received many internal injuries. It was uncertain whether she would survive. I looked at the mother, who with pleading eyes said to me, "Is God punishing us? My daughter can't die. She's everything to me." The father at the same time looked angry and stated, "If you want to pray, pray. I can't believe." A prayer was already forming on my lips as I thought about God's love for this little girl and the tragic events that life sometimes brings our way that are not the will of God. I prayed silently for God to give me the words to convey to these parents that he did not cause this accident to punish them and that he would not abandon them in their distress. I prayed that day with those parents in words that affirmed God's love, that recognized worldly evil, and that let them know that God was present with their daughter during the accident, was with her now as she lay in the bed, and would be with her into the future. By God's grace the little girl survived. Hopefully, an interventional prayer of this type—even if the patient should die—can be used by God to bring assurance of God's love, God's presence, and God's salvation to families and friends who might otherwise question and doubt.

Repentance and Forgiveness

I met Brianna when she stopped me in the hospital hallway and asked if I would do her baptism in the hospital chapel. I sat down with her for a few minutes and sought to understand her request. Brianna was a single mother of two adult daughters who was in the final stages of bone cancer. She was making the decision to be admitted to our comfort care rooms for her final days. She had no local family to take care of her at home, and she knew her body was failing. She wasn't able to live at home anymore. In explaining her request she said, "I grew up in a Baptist church but was never baptized in those early years. Then I got married, had children, divorced, and through it all never really connected with the church again. But God has given me strength through this illness, and I want to be forgiven of my sins." We talked about the gospel message and forgiveness. After a prayer, we set a day for the baptism. I remember that she dressed formally for the occasion and on that day appeared for personal prayer at the chapel before the ceremony. When I arrived she was ready. I read some scripture and baptized her with a bowl of water and a cloth that I squeezed over her head. When the drops ran down her face they mingled with tears of happiness. Brianna said afterward, "I have never had such an emotional experience in my life. A burden has been lifted. I feel so light I could fly! Now I am ready for what comes next." In this last sentence she was speaking of her coming death. I felt very blessed to be a part of God's work in Brianna's life and gifted to see her change of face after the baptism experience.

Over the next weeks I visited Brianna often in her comfort care room and prayed with her as death approached. She asked for Holy Communion several different times and after each experience affirmed how important it was for her faith. Taking the bread and the cup reminded her of forgiveness through Jesus and God's immense love for her. During those weeks she came to terms with the alienation she had experienced from her ex-husband and daughters and at least was able to speak to them long-distance on the phone. To my knowledge, they never made an attempt to visit her before her death. Brianna seemed to understand their issues, however, and would always say to me, "They now know that I love them." When Brianna died I thanked God for this strong woman of faith, who taught me so much about dealing with personal issues and God's grace at the end of our lives. She has become a continued blessing as I remember our friendship and oneness in Christ.

When we come to what we know will be the end of our lives, we often engage in a life review or a life summary. We look back and try to make sense of the totality of the experience and what we have been about and accomplished. Many times there are things we would try to do differently, and sometimes we have deep regrets that haunt us. These regrets can be from relationships or events in which we were involved and for which we are truly sorry. They can also be about sins committed or sins of omission, but in either case the regrets are very disturbing to us. Our most important relationship—the one with our God—is most certainly involved in some way with our life review. Repentance is necessary.

Repentance means "turning back" from something as a result of a "change of mind."[4] Repentance is having "godly sorrow" (1 Cor. 7:10) for sin and a turning around and going in the opposite direction. In the Old Testament, David repented of his sin with Bathsheba when confronted by Nathan the prophet (Ps. 51). In the New Testament, a focus of the message of John the Baptist was "Repent for the kingdom of heaven is near" (Matt. 3:2). Repentance is ultimately an acknowledgment of our human limitations. None of us is perfect. None of us lives exactly as we know we should live. At the end of our lives, the significance of "coming clean" and verbalizing our failures to God and others is important to us.

Repentance also involves confession and forgiveness. "Repentance is never called for without the promise of forgiveness. New Testament writers note that repentance in the deepest sense is beyond human powers. It is both demanded and given. To exercise repentance without hope of forgiveness is a distorted expression of repentance."[5] I think this is why the sacraments are so powerful to us as an assurance of our faith. We take the Eucharist in an attitude of confession, and we are throughout the ceremony assured that forgiveness is gifted to us through the death of our Lord Jesus Christ. Baptism too is, at heart, a confession of human need and confession of our dependence upon Jesus to be Lord of our life. Both sacraments involve repentance and forgiveness and thereby meet a significant and deep-seated human need for reconciliation.

Brianna needed to also have some closure with her children and the years of alienation between her and them. She was, from her side, able to forgive them for their lack of support in her dying days. I don't know the reason behind the distance her daughters had from her. But I do know that Brianna did all she could do to have personal peace in a difficult situation. It was not an easy thing for Brianna to do. Ira Byock notes the difficulty of granting personal forgiveness but compares it to emotional economics. He writes:

> It is wrong to think that people need to feel forgiveness in order to give forgiveness. Forgiveness is actually about emotional economics. It's about a one-time cost that you pay to clear up years of compounded emotional pain. It's like taking a one-time loss in financial investments. Refusing to forgive means accepting the cost of the hurts inflicted on you compounded a thousand times. And it means carrying them forever as they accrue in negative emotional energy.[6]

The need to grant forgiveness is particularly pronounced at the end of our lives, when few other chances may be ours to change a situation or a relationship. When we come to that point it becomes one of life's highest priorities.

To be able to be God's instrument in helping another person with repentance and forgiveness is one of the joys of spiritual advocacy. To listen, to understand, to accept, and to offer verbalized personal forgiveness based upon the promises of scripture is to provide a person with hope and peace at any stage of life.

Hope

All of the various spiritual resources, interventions, and support mechanisms discussed heretofore in this ministry of spiritual advocacy find their culmination in this one word: hope. For to be an advocate in medical decision-making situations, and to act as a resource for persons in difficult ethical dilemmas, *in itself* brings hope to the person or family in crisis. The support roles of presence, listening, prayer, and repentance/forgiveness, along with so many others, all build hope in persons who desperately need a helping hand or an "everlasting arm" to lean upon. The spiritual advocate is a sign of God's workings among his people. The spiritual advocate is an instrument of God's peace in a dry and weary land.

Hope as defined from a Christian perspective involves "looking outside of the self to other resources and promises that can be counted on."[7] Hope becomes a part of our being when we trust that God's promises and purposes will prevail in the end. Holy Scripture builds hope in us as we read historical accounts of God's mighty acts among his people and know that the living God is active and involved in our lives *now*. We are able to trust in God's love and concern for us and "lean not on [our] own understanding" (Prov. 3:5). The Christian experience of hope is found in "learning to live without exclusive reliance on the self."[8] It is found in knowing the promises of God and knowing our value to God. Our ultimate security and safety is guaranteed by our Father in heaven, and so we trust him for our lives.

Given this definition, the spiritual advocate has several means available to strengthen hope in people who need support. First, the reading of God's promises in the Bible is of great encouragement and builds faith and hope (Rom. 10:17). Many Bibles include a topical list of scripture verses for persons who are sick, lonely, fearful, lacking faith, needing guidance, etc. Each spiritual leader no doubt has favorite scripture texts of God's promises that can be recalled even from memory. For example, Psalm 23 is often read at funerals to remind us of God's promise to be our Shepherd as we "walk through the valley of the shadow of death."

Many other scripture verses speak to God's promises for his people and remind us when we hear them that we can have hope in God.

A second means for the advocate to strengthen hope is by reminding the persons in crisis of their positive faith history. We gain strength in times of trouble by remembering that God has seen us through other difficult times in our lives. The advocate can ask the ones needing support to think of another time in their past when a similar situation faced them and of the fact that they survived *then* by God's grace, which brings hope that they will survive now. Such positive faith-history thinking prompts us to call upon our own gifts and personal resources, as well as to rely upon the eventual working of God to bring about a resolution to our difficulties. A third and related means to strengthen hope is by asking the persons in crisis to recall times in their past when they were in mortal danger. Most of us can remember times when we were perhaps close to death, or in a situation that could have resulted in our deaths, but somehow we were protected and lived through the experience. Sometimes such events bring great emotion to us as we recall them. But then we also give thanks to God for "getting us through," and the thoughts and memories can be transferred to the present crisis with the knowledge that God has acted in the past to save us and can act in the future. Hope is the result. The spiritual advocate has facilitated a wonderful blessing for a person when faith in God can be strengthened. Trust in God and hope in God brings glory to his name.

Conclusion

Whether you are a Christian nurse, doctor, church elder, pastor, priest, Bible study leader, neighbor, or just a concerned friend in the faith, God has called you to be a support and advocate for your friends and brothers and sisters in Christ. As a spiritual leader newly aware of this advocacy ministry so needed by persons faced with ethical dilemmas, you have a new calling to minister in situations that may have seemed intimidating in the past. You can be sure that the need is great and that God will open doors for you to support people faced with tough medical decision-making situations. It is my passion and desire to help you grow in this new ministry function of health-care advocacy. To the degree that personal growth in Christian advocacy has been a reality in your life, then this book has been a success.

The disciples of Jesus Christ have entered a new era of responsibility as followers of the Lord of Life. We are called to bring love to bear in situations where life and death meet each other within our local medical center. We must have a new self-awareness of personal issues—theological and emotional—that affect us and the patient families who ask us to accompany them. Into this health-care maze of competing values and ethical dilemmas, a person with a godly calling can bring informed counsel and the presence of the Savior. It is a crucial ministry in today's world.

Notes

1. William V. Arnold, *Introduction to Pastoral Care* (Philadelphia: Westminster, 1982), 41.

2. Gary Sweeten, Dave Ping, and Anne Clippard, *Listening for Heaven's Sake* (Cincinnati: Teleios, 1993), 108.

3. Ibid., 109.

4. Arnold, *Introduction to Pastoral Care,* 51.

5. Ibid., 52.

6. Ira Byock, *The Four Things That Matter Most* (New York: Free Press, 2004), 62–63.

7. Arnold, *Introduction to Pastoral Care,* 63.

8. Ibid., 64.

Appendix

The Hippocratic Oath

I swear by Apollo Physician, by Asclepius, by Health, by Panacea and by all the gods and goddesses, making them my witnesses, that I will carry out, according to my ability and judgment, this oath and this indenture.

To hold my teacher in this art equal to my own parents; to make him partner in my livelihood; when he is in need of money to share mine with him; to consider his family as my own brothers, and to teach them this art, if they want to learn it, without fee or indenture; to impart precept, oral instruction, and all other instruction to my own sons, the sons of my teacher, and to indentured pupils who have taken the physician's oath, but to nobody else.

I will use treatment to help the sick according to my ability and judgment, but never with a view to injury and wrong-doing.

Neither will I administer a poison to anybody when asked to do so, nor will I suggest such a course. Similarly I will not give a woman a pessary to cause abortion. But I will keep pure and holy both my life and my art.

I will not use the knife, not even, verily, on sufferers from stone, but I will give place to such as are craftsmen therein.

Into whatsoever house I enter, I will enter to help the sick, and I will abstain from all intentional wrongdoing and harm, especially from abusing the bodies of man or woman, bond or free.

And whatsoever I shall see or hear in the course of my profession, as well as outside my profession in my intercourse with men, if it be what should not be published abroad, I will never divulge, holding such things to be holy secrets.

Now if I carry out this oath, and break it not, may I gain for ever reputation among all men for my life and for my art; but if I transgress it and forswear myself, may the opposite befall me.

See W. H. S. Jones, *Hippocrates,* vol. 1 (London, 1923), 299–301.